THE FATHERS OF THE CHURCH

SHORTER WORKS

VOLUME 1

THE FATHERS OF THE CHURCH

SHORTER WORKS

ST. GREGORY OF NYSSA

ON THE SIX DAYS OF CREATION

Translated by

ROBIN ORTON

THE CATHOLIC UNIVERSITY OF AMERICA PRESS
Washington, D.C.

Printed in the United States of America

The paper used in this publication meets the minimum requirements of the American National Standards for Information Science—Permanence of Paper for Printed Library Materials, ANSI Z39.48 - 1984.
∞

Cataloging-in-Publication data can be obtained from the Library of Congress.
ISBN 978-0-8132-3376-5

To my daughter, Ann

CONTENTS

ABBREVIATIONS

Full bibliographical details appear in the Select Bibliography if not provided here.

D [number]	Page number in Drobner's edition
Drobner	Drobner's edition of *hex* (GNO vol. IV.I)
Forbes	Forbes's edition of *hex* (1855)
FOTC	Fathers of the Church (The Catholic University of America Press)
GNO	Gregorii Nysseni Opera (Brill edition)
hex	Gregory of Nyssa, *in Hexaemeron*
hom	Basil of Caesarea, *Homiliae in Hexaemeron*
Köckert	Köckert, Charlotte, *Christliche Kosmologie und kaiserzeitliche Philosophie*
Lampe	Lampe, G. W. H., *A Patristic Greek Lexicon* (Oxford: The Clarendon Press, 2004)
Liddell & Scott	Liddell, Henry George, and Henry Scott (revised Sir Henry Stuart Jones), *A Greek-English Lexicon* (Oxford: The Clarendon Press, 1996)
LXX	Septuagint
M [number]	Column number in PG (Migne), vol. 44
NRSV	New Revised Standard Version of the Bible (Catholic edition)
ODCC	Cross, F. L., and E. A. Livingstone, *The Oxford Dictionary of the Christian Church,* Third Edition (Oxford: The University Press, 1997)

PG	Patrologia Graeca, ed. J.-P. Migne
Risch	F. X. Risch, *Gregor von Nyssa, Über das Sechstagewerk*
Way	Way's translation of *hom* (Fathers of the Church 46)

SELECT BIBLIOGRAPHY

Armstrong, A. "The Theory of the Non-Existence of Matter in Plotinus and the Cappadocians." In *Plotinian and Christian Studies* VIII, edited by A. Armstrong, 427–29. London: Variorum Reprints, 1979.

Balás, David. Μετουσία Θεοῦ: *Man's Participation in God's Perfections According to St Gregory of Nyssa.* Studia Anselmiana, Fasciculus LV. Rome: Herder, 1966.

Basil of Caesarea. *Homiliae in Hexaemeron.* Greek text and Latin translation in J.-P. Migne, ed., Patrologia Graeca 29:3–208. Paris, 1857.

———. *Exegetic Homilies.* Translated by Sister Agnes Clare Way. Fathers of the Church 46. Washington, DC: The Catholic University of America Press, 1963.

Bouteneff, Peter. *Beginnings: Ancient Christian Readings of the Biblical Creation Narratives.* Grand Rapids, MI: Baker Academic, 2008.

Corsini, E. "Nouvelles Perspectives sur le Problème de Sources de l'*Hexaéméron* de Grégoire de Nysse." *Studia Patristica* 1.1 (1957): 94–103. Edited by Kurt Aland and F. L. Cross. Berlin: Akademie-Verlag.

Costache, Doru. "Approaching *An Apology for the Hexaemeron*: Its Aims, Method and Discourse." *Phronema* 27 (2012): 53–81.

———. "Making Sense of the World: Theology and Science in Gregory of Nyssa's *An Apology for the Hexaemeron.*" *Phronema* 28 (2013): 1–28.

DeMarco, David C. "The Presentation and Reception of Basil's *Homiliae in Hexaemeron* in Gregory's *Hexaemeron.*" *Zeitschrift für Antikes Christentum* 17.2 (2013): 332–52.

Gregory of Nyssa. *In Hexaemeron.* Greek text edited by Hubertus R. Drobner. Gregorii Nysseni Opera, Opera Exegetica in Genesim, Pars I, vol. IV.I. Leiden: E. J. Brill, 2009.

———. *In Hexaemeron.* Greek text and Latin translation in *Sancti patris nostri Gregorii Nysseni Basilii magni fratris quae supersunt omnia,* vol. 1, edited by George Hay Forbes, 4–95. Burntisland: The Pitsligo Press, 1855. Consulted at http://reader.digitale-sammlungen.de/de/fs1/object/display/bsb10606546_00022.html.

———. *In Hexaemeron.* Greek text and Latin translation in J.-P. Migne, ed., Patrologia Graeca 44:61–124. Paris, 1863.

———. *In Hexaemeron.* German translation, with introduction, notes, and commentary. In Franz Xaver Risch, ed., *Gregor von Nyssa, Über das Sechstagewerk.* Stuttgart: Anton Hiersemann, 1999.

Köckert, Charlotte. *Christliche Kosmologie und kaiserzeitliche Philosophie.* Tübingen: Mohr Siebeck, 2009.

Marmodoro, Anna. "Gregory of Nyssa on the Creation of the World." In *Causation and Creation in Late Antiquity,* edited by Anna Marmodoro and Brian Prince, 94–111 (94–96). Cambridge: The University Press, 2015.

O'Brien, Karl Sean. "Creation, Cosmogony and Cappadocian Cosmology." In *The Ecumenical Legacy of the Cappadocians,* edited by Nicu Dumitraşcu, 7–20. Pathways for Ecumenical and Interreligious Dialogue. Series edited by Mark Chapman and Gerard Mannion. New York: Palgrave Macmillan, 2015.

Sorabji, Richard. *Time, Creation and the Continuum: Theories in Antiquity and the Early Middle Ages.* London: Duckworth, 1983.

van Winden, J. C. M. "The Early Christian Exegesis of 'Heaven and Earth' in Genesis 1." In *Romanitas and Christianitas: Studia I. H. Waszink,* edited by W. den Boer, P. G. van der Nat, G. M. J. Sicking, and J. C. M. van Winden, 371–82. Amsterdam: North Holland Publishing Company, 1973.

von Balthasar, Hans Urs. *Presence and Thought: An Essay on the Religious Philosophy of Gregory of Nyssa.* Translated from the French by Mark Sebanc. San Francisco: Ignatius Press, 1995.

PREFACE

St. Gregory of Nyssa's treatise *in Hexaemeron, On the Six Days [of Creation]*[1]—henceforth *hex*—was one of two works he wrote in response to his elder brother St. Basil of Caesarea's series of nine homilies on the same topic, the *Homilies on the Six Days* (henceforth *hom*).[2] Both of Gregory's two works were addressed to a third brother, Peter. The first was *On the Making of Humankind* (*de hominis opificio*); Basil's *hom* had covered only the creation of

1. The title varies in different mss. I follow the Brill edition—*Gregorii Nysseni in Hexaemeron, Opera Exegetica in Genesim, Pars I,* ed. Hubertus R. Drobner, Gregorii Nysseni Opera, vol. IV.I, Opera Exegetica in Genesim, Pars I (Leiden and Boston: E. J. Brill, 2009), henceforth "Drobner"—which gives it as Γρηγορίου ἐπισκόπου Νύσσης εἰς τὴν ἑξαήμερον. Δημιουργίαν or κοσμογονίαν needs to be understood after the adjective ἑξαήμερον; see Franz Xaver Risch, *Gregor von Nyssa, Über das Sechstagewerk* (Stuttgart: Anton Hiersemann, 1999; henceforth "Risch"), 103, n. 1.

J.-P. Migne, ed., Patrologia Graeca 44 (Paris, 1863; henceforth "PG"), 61–62, calls it an "apologetic by our saintly Father Gregory, Bishop of Nyssa, to his brother Peter, about the six days." Risch says that the designation "apologetic" seems to have been introduced into the ms. tradition comparatively late, but nevertheless he refers to the work throughout as the "Apologia." See section 2 and n. 7 of the introduction for possible "apologetic" elements in *hex.*

2. I have used the Greek text in PG 29:3–208, and, unless otherwise stated, quote the English translation in Saint Basil the Great, *Exegetic Homilies,* trans. Sister Agnes Clare Way, Fathers of the Church 46 (Washington, DC: The Catholic University of America Press, 1963); henceforth "Way." References to passages from *hom* are to the numbered sermons and sections thereof as in PG, which Way follows.

the natural world (Genesis 1.1–24), so Gregory supplemented it with an account of the creation of humankind. The second, *hex,* was ostensibly aimed at dealing with seven particular difficulties that "learned hearers" or Peter himself had raised, either in regard to the Genesis 1 account of the creation of the natural world or in regard to Basil's exegesis of it.

Hom was regarded in later Christian antiquity as the authoritative exposition of Genesis 1.1–24. Already in the later fourth century, St. Gregory of Nazianzus praised it in extravagant terms,[3] and St. Ambrose inserted passages from it into his own treatise on the Six Days.[4] *Hex,* on the other hand, did not become a popular work, although excerpts from it are occasionally quoted by later writers.[5] Doru Costache suggests that the reason for its comparative neglect is that it "distinguishes itself by a scanty theological discourse and almost complete lack of interest in topics pertaining to the spiritual life, by which it remains unique within the Nyssen's literary corpus." The Church "consequently pushed the treatise into oblivion."[6]

It is no doubt on the basis of judgments of this sort that no complete translation of *hex* into English has been undertaken. I believe, for reasons that I shall try to explain in the introduction to my translation, that such judgments are unduly negative about the merits of the work, certainly about its theological interest.

In my translation I have generally followed the text as

3. See Way, viii, where Gregory of Nazianzus, Homily 43, is quoted.

4. Way, ibid.

5. Risch, 47.

6. Doru Costache, "Approaching *An Apology for the Hexaemeron*: Its Aims, Method and Discourse," *Phronema* 27 (2012): 53–81 (59).

edited by Hubertus Drobner in the series Gregorii Nysseni Opera, published by Brill.[7] I have also consulted two other editions: that of George Hay Forbes, the first modern critical edition, published in the nineteenth century,[8] and that in PG,[9] which does not take Forbes's work into account. If for any reason I have decided not to follow Drobner's text, I have explained this in a footnote.

I have made great use of the German translation by F. X. Risch[10] and of his extensive introduction and commentary (the latter in the form of endnotes). I have also consulted the Latin translations in the Forbes edition and in PG. The former, which is a reworking of a sixteenth-century translation by Laurentius Sifanus, sometimes expands the literal meaning of the Greek text for the sake of clarification of the underlying sense. The latter reproduces another sixteenth-century translation, that of Franciscus Zinus, who tends in the opposite direction and sometimes omits short passages (usually difficult ones!).[11] Like Drobner and Risch, I adopt Forbes's division of the text into seventy-eight numbered sections. For ease of reference, I have inserted into the text of my translation the page numbers of Drobner's edition (as D[number]) and the column numbers of PG (Migne) 44 (as M[number]).

Risch sets out his aim of making the translation as literal as possible:

7. See n. 1.

8. *Sancti patris nostri Gregorii Nysseni Basilii magni fratris quae supersunt omnia,* vol. 1, ed. George Hay Forbes (Burntisland: The Pitsligo Press, 1855); consulted at http://reader.digitale-sammlungen.de/de/fs1/object/display/bsb10606546_00022.html. Henceforth "Forbes."

9. See n. 1. *Hex* is contained in columns 61A to 124C.

10. See n. 1.

11. See Risch, 56.

... in order to offer the German reader the opportunity of, at any rate to some extent, appreciating Gregory's rhetoric. I consciously reject the French style of modernizing circumlocution, which derives from belles-lettrists and which is indulged in by the authors of *Sources Chrétiennes.* I accept that here and there this causes problems of readability.[12]

I have taken a rather less purist line and have aimed to steer a middle course between faithfulness to the Greek and the need to present what Gregory is saying clearly and in a modern English idiom. Where the translation significantly departs from a word-for-word rendering of the Greek, I have usually put a more literal version in a footnote. I have not, however, usually drawn attention to the many places where, for the sake of clarity and comprehensibility, I have split up Gregory's long and complicated sentences into shorter ones.

Among the modern works I have made use of in preparing this introduction and the notes to the translation, I wish to express my appreciation in particular of Risch's work and of Charlotte Köckert's *Christliche Kosmologie und kaiserzeitliche Philosophie.*[13] I would not have considered embarking on this book without having them both on my desk beside me.

I would like to thank Professor Markus Vinzent and Professor Tom O'Loughlin, who, at different stages, encouraged me in this project. I am also grateful to King's College, London, who helped me to complete it by awarding me a visiting research fellowship. I would also like to give special thanks to my editor at the Catholic University

12. Risch, 56–57, my translation.

13. Charlotte Köckert, *Christliche Kosmologie und kaiserzeitliche Philosophie* (Tübingen: Mohr Siebeck, 2009); henceforth "Köckert."

of America Press, Dr. Carole Monica Burnett, to whose learning, skill, and wisdom I am greatly indebted.

My daughter Ann is, as it happens, the first cousin, six times removed, of the Revd. George Forbes, of the Scottish Episcopal Church, the first modern editor of *hex* (see above). But that is not the reason I dedicate this book to her, in love and gratitude.

INTRODUCTION

INTRODUCTION

1. Date of Composition

The dates neither of Gregory's *in Hexaemeron* (*hex*) nor of Basil's homilies given the same name (*hom*) can be firmly established. *Hom* has generally been thought to have been delivered before 370, when Basil became a bishop, but could possibly be as late as Lent 378. We know from *hex* §77 that Gregory wrote *de hominis opificio* before *hex*. The tone of *hex* suggests, but does not prove, that it was written after Basil's death, which probably took place in January 379. The fact that in *hex* Gregory addresses his brother Peter as "man of God" (§1) and "Your Perfection" (§77) suggests that Peter was already a bishop; he was elected to the see of Sebaste in Lesser Armenia in 380. In *contra Eunomium* II, written in 380 or the first half of 381, Gregory refers to existing works of his on the subject of Genesis, presumably *de hominis opificio* and *hex*. So 380–381 seems the most likely date for the composition of *hex*.[1]

1. This paragraph draws mainly on Risch, 11–15.

2. The Aim and Genre of the Work

What was Gregory's precise purpose in writing *hex*? Is it possible (or, one might perhaps ask, necessary) to assign the work to a specific genre?[2]

On the face of it, Gregory's aim is to deal with the seven questions, prompted by *hom*, which had been raised by Peter and others (§§3, 5). The questions are as follows:

1. How could day and night have been created (Genesis 1.4–5) before the sun (Genesis 1.14–19)?

2. How can Basil refer to the creation of two heavens when Genesis 1 mentions the creation only of one? And what about St. Paul's "third heaven" (2 Corinthians 12.2)?

3. Why did light, but not darkness, need to be created?

4. If only light was needed in order for the cycle of days and nights to be established, why was it necessary to create the sun? (This is, of course, question 1, put the other way round.)

5. Genesis 1.1 says that the earth was created at the same time as the heavens, but that it was "unformed."[3] What is the difference between "created" and "formed"?

6. If the waters above the firmament (conceived of as a dome) in Genesis 1.6–8 are just like earthly waters, why don't they just flow away down the convex surfaces of the dome?

7. Basil thinks that the waters above the firmament

2. See the discussions in Risch, 49, and Costache, "Approaching *An Apology*," *passim*.

3. Or "in a raw state." See translation, n. 22.

were created in order periodically to "top up" the earthly waters as they are gradually consumed by fire. But is there any evidence to believe that this is in fact happening?

It is clear, however, that Gregory has wider aims, and that the seven questions (or at any rate questions 1–5; questions 6 and 7 are dealt with separately and in great detail, as will be seen later) can be regarded mainly as pegs on which to hang a more extended discussion of the creation. Much of the book is structured, like *hom,* as a more or less sequential commentary on Genesis 1 (or rather parts of it; see later). Drobner's edition classifies it as an "exegetical work" on Genesis. Gregory deals with Peter's seven questions in the order in which they fit naturally into the text of Genesis and his commentary on it, rather than the order in which he had originally set them out.[4]

But the work is clearly more than just a commentary on the text of Scripture. Indeed, there are long passages in which Scripture is hardly referred to. It seems that the Scriptural text too is being used as a peg for Gregory's reflections and arguments about what he calls "philosophy."[5]

4. Gregory addresses the questions in the following sections: question 1 in §§13–14 (creation of day and night); question 2 in §§18 and 24 (identification of the firmament with heaven) and 75 (division of the space under the firmament into different zones); question 3 in §§10 and 13 ("darkness" as the undifferentiated pleroma from which light is separated out; but see translation, n. 20); question 4, as for question 1 and also in §§64–74 (separation out of the heavenly bodies from the primordial light); question 5 in §§16–17 (in its "unformed" state earth exists but only potentially); question 6 in §27; and question 7 in the extended treatment in §§27–63.

5. See the discussion in Costache, "Approaching *An Apology,*" 63–66.

The way the term φιλοσοφία was used in the ancient world is of course very different from the way we use "philosophy" today. Gregory often uses it in *hex* to mean something like "systematic investigation" of a subject. And it needs to be noted that early Christian writers did not consider the Bible as a book in opposition to "philosophy"; on the contrary, they saw it as itself belonging to the realm of "philosophy," like the "wisdom of the ancients" or the "old logos" of the Stoics.[6]

But the sort of "philosophy" with which Gregory is most concerned in *hex* is natural philosophy, what we would now call natural science. One of his principal concerns is to reconcile the Scriptural account of the creation with the ideas about natural philosophy—Platonic, Aristotelian, Stoic, or Neoplatonist in origin—that were current in his day. This can be seen as a form of Christian apologetic, and perhaps explains why the work has traditionally been referred to as an "apologia."[7] It is clear that natural philosophy was something that in any case interested Gregory greatly;[8] indeed, it has been suggested that if he were living today he would have devoted more

6. See J. C. M. van Winden, "The Early Christian Exegesis of 'Heaven and Earth' in Genesis 1," in *Romanitas and Christianitas: Studia I. H. Waszink*, ed. W. den Boer, P. G. van der Nat, G. M. J. Sicking, and J. C. M. van Winden (Amsterdam: North Holland Publishing Company, 1973), 371–82 (371). In §1, Gregory says that in Genesis 1 Moses was expressing a "philosophy of the origin of the world."

7. Risch, 8–9, suggests that the work is "apologetic" also in the sense that Gregory is defending Basil against dissatisfied readers (and is thus an "Apology for the Six Days" in a double sense), and also defending himself against accusations of challenging the supremacy of his brother.

8. See, for example, the long essay on human anatomy and physiology that concludes *de hominis opificio.*

attention to scientific research than to lofty philosophical speculations.[9]

A large part of *hex* is accordingly devoted to "scientific" issues. These are largely confined to matters that would fall today under the disciplines of physics, chemistry, cosmology, astronomy, meteorology, and geography. Gregory does not concern himself with botany, zoology, or anthropology. Peter Bouteneff has even suggested indeed that *hex* is so much focused on these scientific issues that a more appropriate title would be "On Fire, Light, and Especially Water."[10] (Why "Especially Water" will be explained shortly.)

This focus on the physical sciences derives largely from the fact that, despite Gregory's work, like that of Basil, having been given the short title "On the Six Days," in his case this is something of a misnomer. As indicated in the preface, neither Basil nor he discusses the creation of humankind on the sixth day of creation. Moreover, Gregory, unlike Basil, covers only those matters dealt with in Genesis 1.1–10 and 13–19, that is, the first, the second, part of the third, and the fourth days. He does not discuss the creation either of plants, on the third day (verses 11–12), or of animals, on the fifth and sixth days (verses 20–25).[11]

But *hex* is by no means a purely "scientific" treatise. *Pace* Costache (see preface), it also contains a lot of sig-

9. Jean Laplace in *Grégoire de Nysse, La Création de l'Homme,* Sources Chrétiennes 6 (Paris: Les Éditions du Cerf, 2002), 11.

10. Peter Bouteneff, *Beginnings: Ancient Christian Readings of the Biblical Creation Narratives* (Grand Rapids, MI: Baker Academic, 2008), 156.

11. This may be another reason why, as indicated in the preface, Gregory's work was less read in later times than Basil's.

nificant theological and metaphysical material. The former is to be found mainly in the parts dealing with God and creation (discussed in section 5.1 below) and how God's wisdom is substantiated in the "construction" of the world through the process of "sequence" (section 5.3 below); the latter in the discussions of the origin and nature of matter (also discussed in section 5.1 below) although this is probably an area that today would be regarded as falling mostly within the area of physics rather than of metaphysics.[12]

But Gregory does not confuse theological with scientific issues. He does not use theology to fill in alleged gaps in the scientific account of the universe and its origin (as some modern Christian apologists are accused of doing).[13] Rather, he uses science to cast further light on the Genesis account by showing how God's wisdom is demonstrated in the wonderful way in which the world is formed and governed by "sequence."

3. Gregory and Basil

Gregory opens his work with elaborate, fulsome even, tributes to his brother. He seems to attribute to him a degree of divine inspiration of the same order as that giv-

12. Risch, 21, suggests that there is metaphysical content in Gregory's accounts of the coming into being (γένεσις) of the world in §§7–27 and 64–72 and of its permanence (διαμονή) in §§28–63. But he seems to recognize that this is difficult to separate out from natural science: "Der metaphysische und, damit verschränkt, der naturphilosophische Inhalt läßt sich in die zwei großen Bereiche aufteilen des Entstehens der Welt und des Bleibens der entstandenen Welt."

13. See Doru Costache, "Making Sense of the World: Theology and Science in Gregory of Nyssa's *An Apology for the Hexaemeron*," *Phronema* 28 (2013): 1–28 (13).

en to Moses. Moses's account in Genesis is like a grain of wheat, Basil's like the ear that grows from it (§1). Gregory's work is in turn a cutting grafted into the great tree which is Basil's (§2). Later, he claims not to be challenging his brother's views even when his own reasoning leads him to different conclusions. He is merely arguing speculatively and not seeking to lay down dogma or to suggest a definitive exegesis of the Scriptural text (§6). Basil himself did not intend "to prescribe his own theories as laws for his audience but rather that there should be, through his teachings, a way for his disciples to access the truth" (§28).

Gregory's overall approach is in fact very similar to Basil's to the extent that they both aim to produce an interpretation of the Genesis account that takes into account the views of contemporary pagan philosophy. And both say explicitly that they reject allegorical interpretations of Scripture[14] (such as those used by Origen, a theologian who was coming increasingly under suspicion in the later fourth century) and that they are taking the text literally.

Gregory explicitly follows Basil in presenting creation

14. *Hom* 9.1, *hex* §§21, 77. Gregory, however, may be a little disingenuous here. A central pillar of his long argument about the waters above the firmament (questions 6 and 7) is what he calls "homonymy," where different things have the same name (§19), or "catachresis," when "the divine words ... refer to something other than what they normally refer to in Scripture" (§44). Thus God is called a "consuming fire," but is not literally a fire; in the same way, the fact that what is above the firmament is called "water" does not mean it has the same properties as earthly water. Catachresis and allegory are, however, both kinds of metaphors, and the distinction between them is perhaps not quite as clear as Gregory implies. In any case, he shows himself elsewhere quite capable of using elaborate allegorical interpretations of Scripture, as in his (probably later) commentary on the Song of Songs.

as a way for Christians to obtain knowledge of God,[15] but develops this further by, as we shall see, drawing attention to God's wisdom and foresight manifested particularly in the principle of "sequence" (see section 5.3 of this introduction). In that sense, *hex* is a more theological work than *hom.*[16]

Basil finds many opportunities to draw moral lessons from the created world, in particular in his seventh, eighth, and ninth homilies, which deal with the creation of the animals. The animal world provides us with salutary examples of good and bad behavior.[17] God "ordained that all things be written [in the creation story] for the edification and guidance of our souls."[18] Gregory, on the other hand, does not, in *hex,* seek to offer reflections on Christian morality based on the creation story,[19] although this may of course to some extent follow inevitably from the fact that his interests here are more in the material and physical aspects than in the biological or anthropological.

Basil has been unjustly criticized, says Gregory, because he made his discourse simple enough to be un-

15. *Hex* §§4, 8; *hom* 1.7 and 11.

16. See Köckert, 529: "Im Vergleich zu Basilius ist Gregors Kosmologie stärker theistisch geprägt."

17. It is difficult to resist quoting some of these. On the one hand, fish stick virtuously to their allotted habitats and do not invade those of others (*hom* 7.4); the widowed turtle dove virtuously refuses to remarry (*hom* 8.6); and the gratitude of the dog to its master puts to shame any man who is ungrateful to his benefactors (*hom* 9.5). On the other hand, crabs use wicked and deceitful stratagems to prey on oysters (*hom* 7.3), and vipers and sea-lampreys interbreed in "an adulterous violation of nature" (*hom* 7.6). According to Way, xi, these animal fables are drawn especially from Herodotus and Aristotle.

18. *Hom* 9.1.

19. This may be yet another reason for *hex*'s comparative neglect in later times, as Costache suggests (see preface above, p. xiv).

derstood by the unlearned people who listened to his sermons and because he did not set out to satisfy those trained in philosophy (§4). Gregory, on the other hand, discusses many of the "philosophical" issues arising from the creation story in an extensive and detailed way, and it is in those discussions that much of the originality and theological interest of his work is to be found.

There are a number of detailed points on which Gregory takes an approach different from that of his brother; the more significant of these will be mentioned later in this introduction or in the notes to the relevant passages of my translation. There is one specific point, however, on which Gregory clearly felt so strongly that he devotes nearly half of his book[20] to challenging Basil's position. These are the matters raised under the questions 6 and 7 posed at the beginning of the work. Gregory seeks to demonstrate that Basil's theory about the water above the firmament—that it is physical water—is wrong, and that the waters above the firmament are non-material, "the plenitude of intellectual powers" (§§19, 21).

It seems quite possible that part of Gregory's motivation in composing *hex* was the desire to move away from under his brother's shadow and establish himself as his successor as the leading theologian of the Cappadocian school of Nicene orthodoxy. On the other hand, there seems no reason to take otherwise than at face value the highly respectful attitude towards Basil that he expresses in the introduction to *hex*, or to speculate about sibling rivalry.[21]

20. Thirty-seven sections (§§27–63) out of seventy-eight.

21. See the discussions about this in Risch, 8–9, and Costache, "Approaching *An Apology*," 60–63.

4. Gregory's Sources

It is, as usual with the Fathers, difficult to identify the precise sources that Gregory drew on in writing *hex,* apart of course from *hom.* The general scientific framework he uses derives ultimately from Plato (*Timaeus*) and, much more so, from Aristotle, in particular his *Meteorologica* and *De generatione et corruptione.* It almost certainly filtered through to him through intermediate sources such as textbooks and commentaries, in some cases no doubt a whole series of them. Origen, and possibly Philo, may be direct sources. There is also clear Stoic influence; Karl Gronau argued in the early twentieth century that a lost commentary on the *Timaeus* by the Stoic Posidonius (135–51 BCE) lay behind the cosmology of Philo and Origen, and, through them, of Basil and Gregory, but this view is now generally discredited.[22]

5. Gregory's Theological and Philosophical Interpretation of the Creation Narrative

In the rest of this introduction, I shall summarize what seem to be the main points of theological or scientific interest that emerge from *hex.* A more detailed commentary on Gregory's arguments may be found in the notes to the translation.

First, a note on the structure of the work. It may be divided into six main parts. The first (§§1–6) is an intro-

22. For this paragraph, see Risch, 52–55; Köckert, 489–91; and E. Corsini, "Nouvelles Perspectives sur le Problème de Sources de l'*Hexaémeron* de Grégoire de Nysse," *Studia Patristica* 1.1: 94–103, ed. Kurt Aland and F. L. Cross (Berlin: Akademie-Verlag, 1957).

duction. It sets out Gregory's reasons for writing the work and explains its relationship with *hom.* The second (§§7–11) gives an overview of the philosophical and theological principles that underlie Gregory's interpretation of the Genesis account of the creation. The third (§§12–26) interprets Genesis 1.1–10. The fourth and longest (§§27–63) provides a detailed critique of Basil's idea that the waters above the firmament are material; this issue will be dealt with separately in part 6 of this introduction. The fifth part (§§64–76) interprets Genesis 1.14–18. The sixth (§§77–78) is a brief conclusion. My account in this section of Gregory's main arguments aims to be a synthetic one; that is, it does not set them out strictly in the order in which Gregory does.

5.1. God and creation

The initial interesting feature of Gregory's account is the notion—never made quite explicit, but certainly implicit in his argument—that God does not just create the material universe[23] but that he creates it in some

23. Gregory has nothing to say in *hex* about the creation of spiritual beings (although he does, as we shall see, characterize the "waters above the firmament" as "intellectual" in nature and seems to identify them with the angelic world). Nor does he, in Platonic fashion, represent the material world as merely a copy of an intelligible world created earlier; see Risch, 31, and Köckert, 422–23, 542. Basil, on the other hand, (*hom* 1.5) speaks of "a certain condition older than the birth of the world and proper to the supramundane powers, one beyond time, everlasting, without beginning or end," which he identifies with the invisible powers of Col 1.16. (All translations from *hom* in this book are by Way, unless otherwise stated.) See van Winden, 373–75, and Karl Sean O'Brien, "Creation, Cosmogony and Cappadocian Cosmology," *The Ecumenical Legacy of the Cappadocians,* ed. Nicu Dumitraşcu (New York: Palgrave Macmillan, 2015), 7–20, 15.

sense out of himself: *creatio ex Deo* rather than *creatio ex nihilo.*[24] *Creatio ex nihilo,* creation out of nothing, eventually of course became the standard Christian doctrine; it is found as early as the second and third centuries, in Tatian and Tertullian. It offends, however, the standard Greek philosophical principle that "like causes like," and it seems likely that Gregory was conscious of this problem in developing his own account.[25]

Gregory expresses the idea of *creatio ex Deo* in two separate ways. The first is seen in the following passage:

> For the power (δύναμις) is at the same time the will; it considers in advance how beings can come into existence and provides the starting point for the actual existence of what had been thought of, so that, with regard to the creation, one can think at the same time about everything that is of God—his will, his wisdom, his power, and the being of what is (τὴν οὐσίαν τῶν ὄντων).[26]

It should be noted that although I have translated δύναμις as "power" here, it invariably carries the connotation of "ability" or "potentiality." Here we may note in §9 (dis-

24. Köckert, 520, 536. It should be noted that in *de hominis opificio* (PG 44:213C) Gregory says that "the universe took being from nothing" (ἔκ τὲ τοῦ μὴ ὄντος ὑποστῆναι τὸ πᾶν). But in that context "taking being from nothing" can only mean "not taking being from pre-existing matter" (see discussion later in this section and n. 38, which refers to an earlier part of the same passage), and it is not therefore inconsistent with the proposition that creation is *ex Deo.* See Richard Sorabji, *Time, Creation and the Continuum: Theories in Antiquity and the Early Middle Ages* (London: Duckworth, 1983), 194, 294.

25. See Anna Marmodoro, "Gregory of Nyssa on the Creation of the World," in *Causation and Creation in Late Antiquity,* ed. Anna Marmodoro and Brian Prince (Cambridge: The University Press, 2015), 94–111 (94–96).

26. §7.

cussed later), "God laid down the starting points, the causes, and the potentialities (δυνάμεις) of everything that exists ..." In the light of that, we can assume that in this passage Gregory is implying that God's δύναμις (power), which is part of his inner nature, is also a potential, reflected in the δυνάμεις (potentialities) which the natural world manifests in time.[27]

So creation is something that a personal God wills, and his will is identical with both his δύναμις and his wisdom. Together, they constitute God's λόγος, his word or reason (not explicitly the Second Person of the Trinity; see later), and "in our opinion at least, with God, word or reason (λόγος) is work" (§10).[28] So the material universe is "*ex Deo,*" but not in the sense that it is just the last trace of a Plotinian "emanation" from an impersonal One. Rather, it seems that the substantial being of the universe, "the being of what is," is in some sense identical with God's will (and his δύναμις and his λόγος).[29] It has even been said that, for Gregory, the material world is the "substantification" of the divine will.[30]

Nevertheless, Gregory does not draw any pantheistic

27. See Risch, 125–27, n. 85.

28. The idea that God's λόγος and the creative work that flows from it are inseparable goes back to the second-century BCE Jewish apologist Aristobulus of Alexandria; see Risch, 156, n. 137.

29. See Risch, 28, and Köckert, 413, 539.

30. Jérome Gaïth, *La conception de la liberté chez Grégoire de Nysse* (Paris: Libraire Philosophique J. Vrin, 1953). Risch (129, n. 90) cites even more explicit statements from other works of Gregory: from *in illud, tunc et ipse Filius,* Gregorii Nysseni Opera (henceforth "GNO") III.II, 11, l.6, τὸ θεῖον θέλημα ὕλη καὶ οὐσία τῶν δημιουργημάτων ἐγένετο, "the divine will becomes the matter and the substance of the things that are created"; and from *in inscriptiones Psalmarum* II.8, GNO V, 94, l. 8, οὗ (= τοῦ θεοῦ) τὸ πρόσταγμα οὐσία γίνεται, "whose (God's) command becomes substance."

implications from this. He is clear that what he calls nature (φύσις) is autonomous; although it is not independent of God's will or δύναμις, it cannot be in any straightforward way identified with it.[31] As we shall see when we come to discuss Gregory's concept of "sequence," his view of the world is in some sense "scientific," that is, "physical-mechanistic," even though it has a purpose and meaning given to it by God.[32]

One of the most striking features of *hex* is that neither the Second nor the Third Person is allotted any explicit role in creation and indeed that there is no mention in the work either of Christ or of God as Trinity. It has been suggested indeed that on the face of it the concept of God Gregory presents is consistent with Judaic monotheism[33] or even with Stoicism.[34] Gregory often speaks of the λόγος of God, but this always refers either to God's utterance ("Then God said ...") or, as in the passage from §10 cited above, to the divine reason, including his will. For Gregory, God's λόγος in this sense can, however, obviously be seen as in some way fulfilling a similar role in the creation narrative to that of the Second Person of the Trinity in other accounts that draw explicitly on John 1.3, "All things came into being through him." Per-

31. See Köckert, 446 and 541. It may be that, as she suggests elsewhere (520, 523), for Gregory creation, although "from God," is not "from God's nature," with the implication that the transcendent God can operate in immanence without jeopardizing his transcendence.

32. Köckert, 522. Whether this is, as it stands, an intellectually coherent position is of course open to doubt, as is shown by the struggles that modern systematic theologians also have in trying to reconcile the idea of God as a providential creator with science, in their case with modern cosmology and evolutionary biology.

33. Risch, 39.

34. Ibid., 37–38.

haps Gregory was reticent about identifying God's λόγος with the Christ in order to avoid any idea of Arian subordinationism.[35]

The second argument for *creatio ex Deo* starts with the question of how God, an immaterial and spiritual being, could have created a material world without breaching the principle that "like causes like." In *hex* §7 Gregory says:

In order to produce beings, he who can do everything put together, by his wise and powerful will, everything through which matter subsists: lightness, heaviness, compactness, looseness, softness, hardness, wetness, dryness, coldness, heat, color, shape, boundary, spacing;[36] in themselves all these are bare notions (ἔννοιαι) and concepts (νοήματα.) Nothing of these things is in itself matter; rather, matter is produced when they come together (συνδραμόντα) with each other.

So Gregory seems to be rejecting the idea of there being a (created) formless, but in some sense material,

35. As suggested by Köckert, 540–41. Köckert notes that Basil (*hom* 3.2) explicitly identifies God's λόγος with the Only-begotten, who is God's co-worker (συνεργός) in creation, but that even he does not develop the idea very much.

36. διάστημα. "Extension" or "(temporal) interval" would be other possible translations. The *locus classicus* for discussion of Gregory's use of the concept of "spacing" is Hans Urs von Balthasar, *Presence and Thought: An Essay on the Religious Philosophy of Gregory of Nyssa,* trans. from the French by Mark Sebanc (San Francisco: Ignatius Press, 1995), 27–35. Von Balthasar and Risch (131–32, n. 95) argue that διάστημα has a unique role in cosmogony in that it must have been created as a precondition for any world of space and time, whatever other qualities that world may evince; in *in Ecclesiasten* (PG 44:729C), Gregory says that "spacing is nothing other than creation." It seems, however, from the present passage that Gregory is putting it on a par with the other qualities that come together after the initial act of creation to constitute the physical universe; see Köckert, 432.

substrate (ὑποκείμενον) on which form is later imposed—found in Plato's *Timaeus* and, as *materia prima,* in Aristotle and in later Platonists. In other words, he is denying that "matter," as a distinct concept, is a precondition for the corporeal world. Material things (or perhaps the elements that go to make them up) are merely the products of a συνδρομή, a coming together, of abstract, purely "noetic" (intellectual) concepts. Gregory expresses this idea in similar terms in his "On the Soul and the Resurrection" (*de anima et resurrectione*). The characteristics of matter, he says there, are not themselves material; they are principles (λόγοι) or concepts (νοήματα) "comprehended by mind and not by sense-perception." It is "the concurrence and union (συνδρομὴ ... καὶ ἕνωσις) of these with each other" that "becomes a body."[37] A version of the same thought can be found in *hom,* where Basil argues that there is no "nature destitute of qualities, existing without quality of itself" and that if the qualities are removed from some material object, "there will be no substrate (ὑποκείμενον)."[38]

It seems that at any rate in this passage in *hex* (and in the passage from *de anima et resurrectione* referred to above) Gregory is claiming that matter is not a basic ontological concept.[39] Rather, it is the product of the

37. PG 46:121C–124D.

38. *Hom* 1.8, my translation.

39. But it should be noted that Gregory is less clear about this in a passage in his *de hominis opificio* (212D–213A), where on the face of it he seems, unlike Basil, to be positing some sort of ὑποκείμενον. He is trying to prove that matter is not co-existent with God, and, to this end, to show there is no reason why the immaterial God could not have created material objects. The possibility is nevertheless entertained of there being some kind of undifferentiated substrate, ὑποκείμενον, to material objects. "In idea (λόγῳ) each kind of quality is separated from

interaction of various abstract or intellectual principles. There has been much debate among modern scholars as to whether this means that Gregory's metaphysics can be characterized as "idealist."[40] But one can say at any rate that he believed that the ontological basis of material objects was mind—not of course individual human minds, but rather νοῦς as a universal "Intellectual-Principle,"[41] which can be identified, or at any rate intimately associated, with God. One can also note with interest that Gregory's theory has, on the face of it, some similarities to the conclusions of modern physicists, whose investigations into the properties of elementary particles and such concepts as quantum gravity lead them to conclude that matter is far from being part of the basic structure of the universe; what we call "matter" is rather a phe-

---

the substratum (= substrate)." The various characteristics (ἰδιωμάτα) are intelligible (νοητά); "if each of these should be withdrawn from the substratum, the whole idea (λόγος) is dissolved." Sorabji, *Time, Creation and the Continuum,* 292, "doubt[s] if Gregory's reference to a substratum [in this passage] amounts to much." He points out that the substratum must in any case be immaterial (as that is the whole purpose of Gregory's argument) and that "substratum is not a separately conceivable thing" since Gregory argues that "if matter were stripped bare of its qualities, it could in no way be grasped in idea."

40. For discussions about this, see von Balthasar, *Presence and Thought,* 47–50; David Balás, Μετουσία Θεοῦ: *Man's Participation in God's Perfections According to St Gregory of Nyssa,* Studia Anselmiana, Fasciculus LV (Rome: Herder, 1966), 41–42; A. Armstrong, "The Theory of the Non-Existence of Matter in Plotinus and the Cappadocians," in *Plotinian and Christian Studies,* VIII, ed. A. Armstrong, 427–29 (London: Variorum Reprints, 1979). Anticipations of Gregory's notion can be found in Plotinus, Origen, and Porphyry; see references in Sorabji, *Time, Creation and the Continuum,* 292–93, Risch, 24–27, and Köckert, 418–24.

41. Which is how Stephen MacKenna renders νοῦς in his celebrated translation of Plotinus; see Plotinus, *The Enneads,* trans. Stephen MacKenna, abridged with an introduction and notes by John Dillon (London: Penguin Books, 1991).

nomenon produced by abstractions, more specifically, by processes,[42] that can be fully understood only in terms of mathematical functions.[43] But I do not think that "qualities" as such, as Gregory understood them, have a role in modern physics; so it would be inappropriate to suggest that his views are in any sense an anticipation of later scientific developments.

5.2. *How everything began: The laying of the foundations*

The conceptual structure supporting Gregory's account of the creation itself is that there was a "simultaneous laying of the foundations of what exists" in the beginning, and that the world developed by "sequence" from those foundations. This is outlined in §§8–9.

"In the beginning" in Genesis 1.1, Gregory proposes, can be interpreted as "in summary"; indeed, the Hebrew is so rendered by one of its Greek translators. This is not only, thinks Gregory, in the sense that the initial statement that "God created the heaven and the earth"[44] is a "summary" of the succeeding verses, which explain in more detail how heaven and earth actually came into being, but also in the sense that the initial creation of heaven and earth, described in Genesis 1.1, was in itself

42. See Lee Smolin, *Three Roads to Quantum Gravity* (London: Weidenfeld and Nicolson, 2000), 63–64: "... the world is not made of stuff, but of processes by which things happen."

43. See Costache, "Making Sense," 21: "... the 'idealistic' perception that material objects are concatenations of some intelligible concepts ... could be included in the current conversations between theologians and physicists, since the latter acknowledge *information* (in the form of *numerical* values) as constitutive to matter" (emphases added).

44. Singular in the Greek. The New Revised Standard Version (NRSV) has "the heavens and the earth."

a "summary" one. "In the beginning" everything in the universe was created ἀθρόως, "all at the same time."[45] This initial act of simultaneous creation is described as a καταβολή, which can mean a "laying of the foundations," but can also mean "sowing" (as of a seed).[46] "What this 'beginning' of the coming into being of the universe invites us to think is that God laid down the starting points, the causes, and the potentialities (δυνάμεις) of everything that exists collectively and instantaneously" (§9).

The notion of an initial simultaneous creation originated with Philo, and is also found in Origen and Didymus the Blind.[47] As discussed later (section 5.3), Gregory adds the idea of a successive unfolding and emergence of

45. In §64, the initial state of the universe is called a "plenitude," πληρώμα.

46. See §16. "It was as if some seminal power (σπερματικῆς τινος δυνάμεως) to make things come into existence had been sown but there were not yet any individual beings in actuality." On the concept of a "seed" in ancient cosmology, see Köckert, 465–81. The idea of a cosmogenic "seed" is found in several ancient philosophers. The best-known example is the Stoic notion of σπερματικοὶ λόγοι, "seminal principles," although, as Köckert (428) points out, Gregory, unlike the Stoics, is clearly using the concept of "seed" as a simile. It is in the singular and does not imply that each material quality has its own individual "seed," as in the Stoic model. Köckert finds the closest analogy to Gregory in the views attributed by Hippolytus of Rome to a second-century Alexandrian Gnostic, Basilides. Very like Gregory, Basilides identifies the primal seed as a *word* whose emission is a noetic rather than (as for the Stoics) a material event (Köckert, 477–78).

It is interesting that the priest and physicist Georges Lemaître, who in 1931 first proposed the modern version of the theory to which Fred Hoyle later gave the name of the "Big Bang," explained it in popular terms as a "cosmic egg," which obviously reminds one of the cosmogenic "seed" of the ancients. See Harald Sack, "Georges Lemaître and the Origins of the Big Bang Theory" at http://scihi.org/george-lemaitre-big-bang-theory/.

47. See Köckert, 426, and the references in Köckert, 238.

the elements and individual things, of which Genesis 1 gives a narrative account.

In some passages Gregory seems to characterize this primal "seed" and "the starting points, the causes, and the potentialities" that constitute it, as purely intellectual or "noetic." In other words, as would be expected from the considerations described in the previous section, he would have identified its constituents with "the bare notions (ἔννοιαι) and concepts (νοήματα)" of §7—abstract qualities, which would then "come together" to form individual material substances.

This is what we find in §§16–17. In §16, he is discussing Genesis 1.2, where the earth, in the Septuagint version, is described as "invisible and unformed" (ἀόρατος καὶ ἀκατασκεύαστος):

"The earth," [Moses] says, "was invisible and unformed," which is equivalent to saying that it both existed and did not exist; for there were not yet any qualities associated with it. The proof of this view is that the text says the earth was invisible. What can be seen is color; color is a sort of emanation of the shape as it appears to the sight; and there can be no shape without a body. So if the earth was invisible, it was altogether without color; being without color, it must be thought of as without shape; without shape, it must be considered as without a body. So in the simultaneous laying of the foundations of the world (ἐν τῷ ἀθρόῳ τῆς τοῦ κόσμου καταβολῆς), the earth was included in the things that are—as indeed was everything else. But it awaited the effect of the provision of qualities; that is what constitutes actually coming into existence. So when the account says the earth was "invisible," it is showing that no other quality was to be observed in it; and when it calls it "unformed," it is inviting us to think that it had not yet become solid by virtue of its corporeal qualities.

In §17, Gregory goes on to make it clear that although the earth was formed from a primal ὑποκείμενον, without individual qualities of its own, that ὑποκείμενον was in no sense material. It was in fact an undifferentiated *mixture of qualities,* the potential state from which individual being will emerge. It is like a seed, which is not the material ὑποκείμενον for the living creature, but rather the potential that develops into it:[48]

> ... in actuality the earth did not actually exist but possessed existence only potentially, and ... each of its qualities was not yet separated from the others and could not be individually recognized. Instead, the totality was perceived in a confused and indistinct quality; neither color nor shape nor bulk nor weight nor size nor anything else of that kind could be observed as it was in itself, according to its own rational principle, within the substrate (ἐν τῷ ὑποκειμένῳ).

There are, however, other passages in which Gregory appears to be characterizing the primal καταβολὴ as material, rather than purely noetic, in nature. In §10, he describes how light emerges from the darkness, as in Genesis 1.2–3:

> For this reason, when the totality of things (τὸ ὅλον) came into being, before anything that formed part of that totality came into view, darkness submerged everything. The brightness of fire, hidden in the constituent parts of matter (τοῖς μορίοις τῆς ὕλης), had not yet appeared. It was like when pebbles remain invisible in the darkness; they have by nature within themselves the power to cause light, by colliding with each other and producing fire; so when a spark appears from them, they too appear visible because of that illumination. In the same way, all

48. See Risch, 175, n. 186.

things were invisible and obscure until the nature that causes light came forth into visibility. Everything had just come into being without any differentiation, all at once in a single decisive action (ῥοπῇ) of the divine will, with all the elements jumbled up together (πεφυρμένων); fire was dispersed everywhere, but was darkened by the superior power of the matter, which obscured it.

This clearly implies that the initial "totality of things," in which "the brightness of fire [was] hidden," was material,[49] and that what were "jumbled up together" in the initial "seed" were not abstract qualities, but material elements. A similar view seems to be expressed in §13, where the context is again Genesis 1.2–3: "What was ... obscured by the matter of the other elements was overshadowed, and the overshadowing was darkness." And in §73, when discussing the emergence of the heavenly bodies on the fourth day of creation, Gregory again seems to refer to the material nature of the primal "mixture":

> ... for by the power of the Creator everything was established simultaneously in material form (ὑλικῶς); then in order to bring actual things into existence, the individual manifestation (ἡ μερικὴ ... ἀνάδειξις) of the objects we see in the universe was completed in a certain natural order and sequence, according to the prescribed interval of time.

So it must be concluded that there is an ambiguity in Gregory's account of the initial καταβολή. Is he a consistent idealist for whom matter is a redundant concept

49. Too much should not perhaps be made of the analogy of (material) stones striking against each other to cause sparks (which recurs in §12). It is only an analogy and need not in itself be taken as implying that Gregory believed the initial emergence of light was due to a similar process.

and for whom what we call individual material substances are not composed of something that can be separately identified and called matter but can be explained as epiphenomena arising from particular combinations of various abstract concepts? Or does he envisage an undifferentiated material "substrate," with individual qualities in some unexplained way remaining "potential" within it, perhaps as an intermediate stage between the purely spiritual God who creates the abstract qualities and the creation of material substances such as the four elements and individual material bodies? No clear answer can be given, and Gregory's account can be reasonably accused of inconsistency.[50]

5.3. The "construction" of heaven and earth

Gregory goes on to explain how, following the initial καταβολὴ, the heaven and earth, and everything they contained, came into existence, as described in Genesis 1.3 and the rest of that chapter. The process is described

50. One of the qualities that material objects need in order actually to exist, set out in §7, is διάστημα, "spacing" (spatial or temporal), on which see n. 36 above. It is difficult for us to imagine a "substrate" that was material but without "spacing," that is, which did not yet exist in space and time. Von Balthasar, *Presence and Thought,* 28, seems to offer a way through this by claiming that Gregory, in his doctrine of creation, gave some sort of precedence to διάστημα over other abstract qualities. It is "the intimate substance of [finite] being" and is necessarily "linked to the idea of creation itself." He quotes *in Ecclesiasten homiliae* to the effect that "spacing is nothing other than creation." If διάστημα was indeed created in some way prior to other qualities, that might provide Gregory with a way of defending an idea of a material substrate (with διάστημα but no other qualities) as an intermediate stage between the καταβολὴ and the creation of individual substances, without abandoning his "idealist" notion of matter. But there is nothing in *hex* to support this. See the discussion in Köckert, 432.

variously as ἀπεργασία, "production";[51] τελείωσις, "completion";[52] κατασκευή[53] or διασκευή,[54] "construction"; and ἀνάδειξις, "manifestation."[55] What existed only potentially comes into actual existence.

There are three passages where Gregory explains how this happens. The key concept is that of "sequence," for which Gregory uses, more or less interchangeably,[56] the terms ἀκολουθία ("sequence"), εἱρμός ("order"), and τάξις (literally, "arrangement").[57]

The first passage is in §9:

[God's] power and wisdom are laid down as foundations (συγκαταβληθείσῃ, etymologically related to καταβολὴ), and a certain necessary order (εἱρμός) follows on (ἐπηκολούθημεν), according to a certain sequence (τάξιν), with a view to bringing to completion (τελείωσιν) each part of the world. One particular thing [that is, light or fire, Genesis 1.3], therefore, of those things that can be seen in the universe, comes first and appears first, and so what necessarily follows after what comes first, and then the third, as nature the artificer (ἡ τεχνικὴ φύσις) requires; then the fourth and the fifth and the rest according to a sequence (ἀκολουθίας), one following on from another. These do not appear as they do by spontaneous chance (οὐκ αὐτομάτῳ τινὶ συντυχίᾳ), through some unordered or accidental process. Each thing came to be, [Moses] says, just as the necessary or-

51. *Hex* §7.
52. *Hex* §9.
53. *Hex* §24.
54. *Hex* §72.
55. *Hex* §64.
56. See Köckert, 440.
57. Gregory may be hinting in §1 at the centrality of this concept to *hex* when he says that Peter has asked him to bring the account of the creation "into logical order (εἱρμὸν), through a process of sequential thinking" (διά τινος ἀκολούθου διανοίας).

der (τάξις) of nature requires a sequence (ἀκόλουθον) among things as they come to be; he uses the form of a narrative to give a philosophical account of theories of natural science, and sets out certain words of command from God as a preliminary to each thing that comes into being. He is acting rightly and piously when he does this. For everything that comes into being according to order (εἱρμόν) and wisdom is an individual direct utterance (φωνή) by God.

In the second passage, in §11, Gregory explains how this process is related to the expression "God said," which precedes the account of individual stages of creation in Genesis 1:

So since the expression "God said" suggests word or reason (λόγου παραστατική ἐστιν ἡ τοιαύτη φωνή), the pious way, in my view, for us to think about it is for us to apply that utterance to the word or reason that lies within creation. For the great David also explained such expressions to us in a similar way, when he said, "In wisdom you have made everything." For the utterance that commanded the creation of what exists, recorded by Moses as an expression of God, is what David called the wisdom that can be seen in what has come into being.... [T]he wisdom that is seen in creation is "word" (λόγος), even if not articulated.

This is further explained in §64:

But it is now time to turn our consideration to the other matter we are inquiring into, how after the third day all the lights of the heaven were made. A particular word of command from God brings about each of these wonderful events (Moses teaches us about these lofty doctrines through the medium of a historical account), as we have established in our earlier arguments. Through those arguments we came to know that the voice of God is not a command expressed through words, but that the word of God is that wise artisanal power found in everything that has come into existence, through which the wonders of existence are given effect, and that it should be spoken of in that way. And we have come to know that everything was constituted simultaneously, in the plenitude of creation (τοῦ κατὰ τὴν κτίσιν πληρώματος), by God's initial will, and that the ordered series (τάξις) that necessarily arose, in consequence of the wisdom that is found within everything that exists, brought each of the elements into its manifestation (πρὸς τὴν ... ἀνάδειξιν) as a consequence (ἀκολουθίαν) of the divine commands. Moses was indicating the totality when he summarized it in an inclusive expression referring to the original coming into existence of the sensible creation: "In the beginning God created the heaven and the earth." He says that God created the sum total (πλήρωμα) of things; he indicates in his account that the manifestation of each existing thing happened in a naturally ordered series (τάξει τινὶ φυσικῇ).

We learn from these passages that "sequence" is at one level a natural physical process, brought about by "nature the artificer." But it is not mechanistic and purposeless, operating "by spontaneous chance, through some unordered or accidental process";[58] it is consequent upon an "individual direct utterance by God" (§9). It is in fact the voice of God that is the "wise artisanal power found in everything."[59] "God said" in Genesis 1 is not to be taken as history; the divine utterance "is not a command expressed through words," even though "Moses teaches us about these lofty doctrines through the medium of a his-

58. Although Gregory could be said to teach a form of evolution, it is far from Darwin's concept of random and mindless natural selection over long periods of historical time.

59. See Köckert, 439–43, for anticipations of these concepts in Stoicism and Neoplatonism, in Galen, and in Philo.

torical account" (§64). Rather, God's λόγος "lies within creation"; it is "the wisdom that can be seen in what has come into being" (§11).

At the concrete "physical" level, the "construction" of the heaven and earth, as set out in Genesis 1, was, in Gregory's view, based on two principles. The first was the emergence of the elements of fire, water, earth, and air from the primal mixture by a process of διάκρισις or separation.[60] (Gregory seeks to explain in §25 why the Genesis account does not specifically refer to the creation of air.) The second is the principle that "like is attracted to like,"[61] which explains how individual particles (μόρια)[62] of a particular element come together to form, for example, the seas and the heavenly bodies. In §§72–73 Gregory gives a general overview of these processes and in §74 provides an analogy for them: water and quicksilver can be mixed together, but the respective individual particles will soon separate and then come together to form separate masses of each substance.

Gregory uses this separation/aggregation model to show how the principle of "sequence" applies to the various acts of creation described in Genesis 1. In §§10, 13, and 65 he deals with the initial emergence of fire

60. See Risch, 34–35, for "Diakrisis-Kosmogonie" as a development of Platonist and Stoic ideas, first attested in the first century BCE.

61. See Risch, 35–36, and Köckert, 462–63. This principle of like being attracted to like is an important element in Gregory's cosmological scheme. It goes back to Empedocles; see G. S. Kirk and J. E. Raven, *The Presocratic Philosophers: A Critical History with a Selection of Texts* (Cambridge: The University Press, 1962), 344, text 459.

62. Risch, 27, calls this terminology "irgendwie atomistisch," but, as Köckert, 457, n. 246, points out, there is no reason to see here any suggestion of Democritean atomist theory. A "particle" is just a (small) "part (μόριον)" of an element.

and light (which he in effect identifies with each other) from the initial "plenitude," as in Genesis 1.3. In §26, he describes how earth and water were separated out from each other and how the seas were formed, as in Genesis 1.9–10. In §66 he describes how the sun, moon, and stars were separated out from the primal, generic light, as in Genesis 1.14–19.

6. Water

As already indicated, Gregory devotes nearly half of *hex* to discussing one particular issue on which he differs radically from Basil, that is, the nature of the water "above the firmament (στερέωμα)"[63] in Genesis 1.6–7. Much of this discussion is quite technical and sometimes difficult to follow. Moreover, its subject matter is almost wholly concerned with natural philosophy and has little obvious direct theological relevance. It may well be that these are some of the reasons for the relative neglect in later times, up to and including today, of *hex* as a whole. Nevertheless, Gregory's ingenious speculations will not, I hope, be without interest for modern students with an interest in the history of science.

6.1. Basil's account of the "waters above the firmament"

For Basil, the firmament is not to be identified with the "first heaven," whose creation is described in Genesis 1.1.

63. "Firmament" is a word that was introduced into English specifically to represent the Vulgate's *firmamentum* in this passage; the Latin word was in turn chosen to translate the LXX στερέωμα. See the Oxford English Dictionary (https://www.oed.com/), s.v. The NRSV renders the Hebrew as "dome."

It is a "second heaven," the sky,[64] "of a more solid nature and furnishing a special service for the universe";[65] it has to be "capable of supporting the fluid and unstable water" above it. Basil deliberately avoids speculating on exactly what it is composed of, but "it seems to have had its origin ... from water."[66]

So Basil interprets these verses in a straightforward way, one which takes Scripture in its natural "Hebraic" way: the water above the firmament really is water, in the same way as the water below,[67] and is the source of precipitation: "When ... Scripture says that the dew and the rain are brought from the heavens, we understand that they are from the waters that are appointed to occupy the region above."[68] He criticizes those who "have recourse to allegories" and say that the waters above signify "spiritual and incorporeal powers" of an "intellectual nature," while "the waters under the heavens" are the "spirits of malice," characterized by "the instability and inconstancy of their voluntary movements."[69] In answer to the objection that if the firmament, that is, the sky, is indeed like a dome or the top half of a sphere (as would be universally assumed in ancient cosmology), and if the water above the firmament is physical water, the latter would simply flow away, Basil responds that even if the inner surface of

64. Gn 1.8: Καὶ ἐκάλεσεν ὁ Θεὸς τὸ στερέωμα οὐρανόν (LXX). NRSV translates the corresponding Hebrew text as "God called the dome Sky."

65. *Hom* 3.3.

66. *Hom* 3.4. Elsewhere he says that its nature is not like the earth, "solid and firm (ἀντίτυπον καὶ στερέμνιον) with weight and resistance" (*hom* 3.7, my translation).

67. *Hom* 3.9, 9.1.

68. *Hom* 3.8.

69. *Hom* 3.9. See also *hom* 2.4.

the dome is smooth, the upper side could well be flat, as it is in some buildings with domed ceilings.[70]

Basil explains why God found it necessary to create real material water above the firmament. At the End, "there will be a time when all things will be burnt up by fire"[71]—although Basil is careful to distance himself from those who "introduce infinite destructions and regenerations of the world,"[72] that is, from the Stoics who believed in a succession of worlds, each ending in a conflagration (ἐκπύρωσις) from which the next world subsequently emerged.[73] But this eschatological conflagration must not happen prematurely. If God had made equal quantities of each of the elements, fire, as the most powerful of them, would soon have consumed all the rest. So God created a reservoir above the firmament containing just enough water to top up (through precipitation) the water below, making up for that which had been consumed by fire (that is, as a result of evaporation caused by the heat of the sun or by the burning hot ether of the upper atmosphere), until the time appointed for the End has arrived and fire no longer needs to be restrained.[74]

6.2. *Gregory's account*

Gregory does not find Basil's account at all satisfactory. He assumes that water as the heaviest element would

70. *Hom* 3.4. Presumably the flat roof would need to have some sort of parapet round it to keep the water from flowing out!

71. *Hom* 3.6.

72. *Hom* 3.8.

73. See Risch, 7, and Köckert, 513, who rebut Corsini's view ("Nouvelles Perspectives," 96–103) that Basil accepts (and Gregory seeks specifically to challenge) the Stoic doctrine.

74. Basil sets all this out at considerable length in *hom* 3.5–8.

sink to the lowest possible place.[75] In §27 he mocks the suggestion that this principle could be met if the upper side of the firmament were intersected by valleys into which the water flowed down to form lakes, like those on earth. (Perhaps he has invented this suggestion to avoid having directly to attack Basil's alternative idea, which he does not mention, that the firmament might have a flat roof.) In any case, he points out that the supposed lakes on the upper side of the firmament would need to have lids on them to stop the water flowing out "when the cyclical revolution of the sphere of heaven brings down below what is now above"!

But in §§28–32 he raises more fundamental objections, which he expresses with all due deference, to Basil's idea that that one element, fire, is more powerful than the rest and "consumes" the other elements. Fire and water are, he concedes, naturally opposed to each other and indeed can, as it were, inflict temporary defeats on each other, to the extent of making each other temporarily disappear: water will quench a fire, and heat will dry water up. But they were created in fixed quantities at the outset, which remain unchanged throughout the history of the universe:

> Earth is a "beautiful and good"[76] thing; it does not need the destruction of air in order to be earth, but continues in its own qualities by virtue of the natural power from God that is contained within it and which is able to preserve itself. Air is a "beautiful and good" thing, not because it is not earth, but

75. See O'Brien, "Creation, Cosmogony and Cappadocian Cosmology," 11.

76. Καλόν, as in Gn 1.10; for the translation, see n. 80 on translation of §12.

because, through the powers that it naturally has within it, it has what it needs in order to continue to be. So too water is "very beautiful and good," and fire is "very beautiful and good," each brought to fulfillment in its own individual qualities and able to stay continually in existence by the power of the divine will according to the measure established for it in the original creation. It is said that "the earth stands forever," without decrease or increase. Air is kept within its own boundaries, fire does not diminish; why, of all these, is it only water that is consumed away? (§31)[77]

Thus in Gregory's model of the universe there is no need for any extra supply of water stored above the firmament. He denies (§§43–44) that there is any reason to believe that the references in the Scriptural account of Noah's flood to the opening and closing of the windows of the heavens[78] are necessarily evidence for any such store of water; nor is there any mention of the firmament being pierced when "through Elijah's prayers, a cloud arose from the sea, and opened heaven for them in the heavy downpour of rain."[79] (Basil does not cite either of these passages in support of his interpretation.)

Gregory needs therefore to explain what Scripture in fact means by the waters above the firmament. He sets

77. See also §62: "And so the cyclical transformation of the elements into each other is continuous and unimpeded; none of them is either consumed or added to, but rather they each continually remain in the quantities measured out for them in the beginning." Köckert, 513–16, cites a number of other ancient philosophers, including some Stoics, who held that the four elements naturally maintained an equilibrium in an eternal chain of mutual transformation: Philo, "Timaeus of Locri" (probably in fact an unknown Middle Platonist), the pseudo-Aristotelian *de mundo,* Cicero, and Seneca.

78. Gn 7.11, 8.3.

79. 1 Kgs 18.44–45.

out his own theory in §§18–23. The firmament is the highest part of the (lower) world of matter and sense; beyond it is the (upper) intellectual world. It is itself material but only just so—imperceptible to the senses, rather than a solid and hard barrier.[80] The waters above the firmament, on the other hand, are purely noetic in nature. It is they that the supernatural light of the Spirit sweeps over (and illuminates) in Genesis 1.2; they do not need the created light of Genesis 1.3.

This notion that the waters above the firmament are "spiritual" rather than material goes back to Origen, but both Basil[81] and Gregory (§21) reject the Origenists' "allegorical" reading,[82] which equates the waters below the firmament with the fallen spirits and those above with the angels. But in §19 Gregory does himself identify the waters above the firmament with "the plenitude of intellectual powers"; he does not explain this further, but is presumably referring to the angels and the powers of heaven described in Colossians 1.16.[83]

Gregory gives a lengthy scientific account in §33–63 of how the world can in fact operate without there being a reserve supply of water to top up that which is consumed

80. This material but imperceptible substance is close to Aristotle's concept of ether; see Köckert, 451.

81. *Hom* 3.9.

82. See Köckert, 385–89. See n. 14 above on the question whether Gregory has in fact totally excluded allegory from his own interpretative method.

83. As Köckert, 485, points out, Origen draws a moralistic distinction between the world above the firmament, guided by reason, and that below, driven by passion. Gregory's distinction between the two kinds of waters is an ontological rather than a moral one, although in the third sentence of §19, there does seem to be an implied connection between evil and the darkness of the waters under the firmament.

by fire. He does this by explaining, with observations from meteorology and geography, how water, fire, and earth are sequentially transformed into each other in a regular cycle—a version of what we now call the "water cycle."

6.3. Gregory's explanation of the "water cycle"

The conceptual framework that Gregory uses in his account is described in §§29–30, 38–41, and 53–57.[84] It is based on (without exactly following) Aristotle's notion, set out in his *de generatione et corruptione* 2.3–4, that each of the four elements is formed from a combination of two of four fundamental qualities, one of which can be characterized as the dominant one. For Aristotle, fire is hot (dominant) and dry; air is wet (dominant) and hot; water is cold (dominant) and wet; earth is dry (dominant) and cold. When any quality is "overcome," that is, eliminated, by its opposite, one element is transformed into another; thus, in fire, if the dryness is "overcome" by the wetness of water, the fire becomes air, which retains fire's heat but not its wetness. This gets more complicated in the conversion of earth into air (or vice versa) or of fire into water (or vice versa) when both of the qualities of each element have to be "overcome." In this case, a third, intermediate element needs to be introduced into the cycle. For example, if fire is added to water, air and earth are produced: the air takes heat from the fire and wetness from the water, and the earth takes coldness from the water and dryness from the fire.

The role of the *qualities* in bringing about the transfor-

84. I draw extensively from Köckert, 505–9, in the following paragraphs.

mation of elements in Aristotle's scheme was no doubt attractive to Gregory because it seemed consistent with his notion that a non-material God created non-material qualities rather than an undifferentiated material substrate (§7).[85] But he introduces some changes into that scheme.

First, like many post-Aristotle philosophers, he considers that air is cold and wet rather than hot and wet (see §§55 and 56). As this makes both water and air cold and wet, he has to introduce the additional qualities of lightness and heaviness (§41) to distinguish between them.[86] Secondly, he modifies Aristotle's scheme by introducing the idea that elements are transformed into each other by virtue of the common quality that they share; the non-dominant quality of the first becomes the dominant quality of the second. This enables him to say that earth potentially contains water because its non-dominant quality, cold, is the dominant quality of water (§56). Fire (hot, dry) and air (cold, wet) can be transformed into each other because they have "lightness" as a common quality (§55).

Gregory uses this theoretical underpinning to explain the water cycle and to show how it removes the need for any source of water outside the celestial sphere. Because of the sun's heat, water dries up, becomes vapor (or, according to §62, is transformed into air) because of the sun's heat, and forms clouds (§§33–34). Much of it returns to the earth as precipitation and is then drawn back up to the clouds in a continuous cycle (§§35–38),

85. As pointed out by Köckert, 520.
86. See Köckert, 506 and n. 448.

but none of it actually ceases to exist. Some particles of vapor do not form precipitation, however, but lose their properties of wetness and coldness and retain only that of weight—a bit like what happens when (wet) oil burning in a lamp is transformed into (dry) soot (§§39–41, 43, 46). Tiny, usually imperceptible, particles of what is, in effect, earth are formed and fall back to the earth, into which they are reabsorbed (§§47–49). Then earth takes its place in the cycle; the cold, dry earth is transformed into cold, wet water, which comes back to the surface through springs and wells and re-enters the water cycle (§§56–62). Although all the elements are forever changing into each other in a constantly repeated cycle, there is no net increase or decrease in the quantities in which they were originally created. So there is no need for a spare supply of water above the firmament.

ON THE SIX DAYS OF CREATION

ON THE SIX DAYS OF CREATION

WHY DO YOU do this, man of God?[1] Why do you tell us to dare something that should not be dared, to embark on a project of a kind for which not only is success unachievable but which it is [D6], at any rate in my view, reprehensible even to embark upon? You enjoined us to bring into logical order,[2] through a process of sequential thinking,[3] those parts of the philosophy of the origin of the world expressed, through divine inspiration, by the great Moses that, on a superficial reading of the text, appear contradictory, and to show that the Holy Scripture is internally consistent. You asked us to do the same for the divinely-inspired study[4] of this material by our father,[5] by which

1. The text begins at D5 and M61 in Drobner and Migne, respectively. The abrupt beginning and the rest of the introduction (§§1–6) incorporate a classical rhetorical device: "benevolum, attentum, docilem facere" (Risch, 20, referring to Quintilian, *institutio oratoria,* 4.1.5). The "man of God" is Gregory's brother Peter, bishop of Sebaste; see introduction, part 1, p. 3.

2. εἴς εἱρμὸν ἀγαγεῖν. εἱρμός is an important word in *hex,* as is ἀκολουθία / ἀκόλουθος; see next note, n. 57, and introduction, part 5.3, p. 26.

3. διὰ τινος ἀκολούθου διανοίας: see previous note.

4. τὴν θεόπνευστον … θεωρίαν. Gregory is putting Basil on almost the same level as Moses himself; see David C. DeMarco, "The Presentation and Reception of Basil's *Homiliae in Hexaemeron* in Gregory's *Hexaemeron,*" *Zeitschrift für Antikes Christentum* 17.2 (2013): 332–52 (335).

5. Spiritual father.

all those who know it are amazed, no less than by the philosophy expressed by Moses himself. Rightly so, I think. One could say that the relationship between the voice of the great Moses and the thoughts worked out by the great Basil by more laborious study is like that between the grain seed and the ear. The latter comes from the former; it is not identical with it but can be said to be the same thing in terms of its potentiality;[6] it is changed in size, beauty, color, and shape. [D7, M64] What Moses said in a few well-chosen words our teacher extended by lofty philosophy.[7] He made not an ear but a tree, like the mustard seed that is compared to the kingdom and grows into a tree in the heart of the farmer.[8] It spreads out its thoughts on all sides and, instead of branches, unfolds doctrines; it stretches itself upward with piety as its objective, so that the lofty and high-flying souls, which the Gos-

6. "Potentiality" is τῇ δυνάμει. Throughout I translate δύναμις as either "potential/potentiality" or "power," depending on the context. See introduction, part 5.1, pp. 14–15.

If Gregory is referring to the Aristotelian distinction between potentiality (δύναμις) and actuality (ἐνέργεια), it is odd that he seems to be attributing potentiality to the ear rather than to the seed. Risch (110–11, n. 14) and Köckert (402) suggest (following van Winden) that this is because both the seed and the ear have "vegetative power." DeMarco, "Presentation and Reception," 336–37, argues, on the other hand, that to say that the ear continues to possess the δύναμις that it had as a seed is not inconsistent with Aristotelian usage.

7. I think DeMarco, "Presentation and Reception," 337, is right to interpret Gregory as implying that Basil's writings are indeed in some respect superior to those of Moses; they are not more authoritative, but are fuller and more detailed because they bring out the scientific and moral implications of the Scriptural text.

8. This seems to assume that "his field," into which the farmer sowed the mustard in Mt 13.31, represents his own heart, i.e., that the farmer stands for him who receives the Gospel rather than him who preaches it.

pel calls the birds of the air,[9] can make a nest in the great quantity of its branches. The resolution of the question at issue is like a nest for the soul; it provides a rest for the ceaseless busy activity of the mind, which is like a solitary flight wandering far and wide.

2. How then is it possible for us to plant that little cutting that is our thinking next to such and so great a tree of words? Surely[10] you are not telling me—indeed I would not agree to it—to set up our work in opposition to the devoted labors of our father and teacher! Rather, it is like the wonders that farmers do [D8] when they cleverly produce different fruits from one plant. This is how they do grafting. They tear away a short shoot[11] from one tree, together with the bark at its base, and fit the bark into a certain part of an incision in another, larger plant. Thus the inserted shoot is nourished by the natural moisture of the greater tree and grows up into a branch. In the same way I shall myself join my understanding like a short stalk to the moisture of the great tree, the wisdom of our teacher, and seek to become a branch of it. So far as it is possible for me, I shall implant myself into his thoughts and irrigate myself with the abundance of the supplies which are given to us from that source.

3. I myself think that some people have not properly recognized the aim of his labors on the six days. So, in the first place, they blame him for not having given them clear information about the sun, about how that radiant object could have been made after three days with

9. Mt 13.32.

10. Reading ἦ with Risch (112, n. 23) rather than ἤ with PG, Forbes, and Drobner.

11. φύλλυν, literally "leaf."

the other stars, since it would have been impossible for the span of each day to be separated into morning and evening unless the sun had made [D9] the evening by setting and the morning by rising.[12] Then again, they do not accept the creation of the two heavens;[13] the fact that the Apostle[14] mentions a third heaven as well does not, they say, reduce the difficulty on this point. One heaven came into existence "in the beginning"[15] and then, later, the firmament; Moses did not record the creation of another heaven. So it cannot be proved that one can think of a third heaven over and above these two. No other one came into existence after the firmament, nor is it consonant with the concept of "the beginning" to think of something older. For if the heaven came into being "in the beginning," it was clearly from then that creation began. For it would not have been called "beginning" by Scripture if it had another "beginning" lying beyond it; what comes second in a series is not the "beginning,"

12. Basil says (*hom* 2.8) that the division between day and night was originally not "according to solar motion" (κατὰ κίνεσιν ἡλιακὴν) but that "light was diffused and drawn in again according to the measure ordained by God." Later (6.2) he suggests that the sun was created after day and night "lest men might call the sun the first cause and father of light and lest they who are ignorant of God might deem it the producer of what grows from the earth"; see also 5.1. Gregory gives an elaborate "scientific" explanation of his own in §§67–74.

13. Basil (3.3) admits the possibility of innumerable heavens, but in any event explicitly distinguishes the heaven of Gn 1.1 from the "second heaven," that of Gn 1.8, the firmament. (N.B. that they are both οὐρανὸν in LXX; NRSV translates the Heb. as "sky" in Gn 1.8.)

14. Paul, in 2 Cor 12.3.

15. The syntax suggests that here and in the rest of this section Gregory is speaking for himself rather than representing the views of Basil's critics. Later (§§75–76) he says that there is no need to posit any particular number of heavens, as Scripture can use the word in different senses in different places (see the example in n. 13 above).

nor can it be called so. But Paul mentions a third [M65] heaven too, which is not spoken of in the creation narrative; in that context too an account of the second is something that needs asking about.

4. Those who advance these points, or ones like them, seem to me not to consider the objective of our father's teaching. [D10] He spoke to such a large number of people together in a crowded assembly that he necessarily made his discourse suited to those who were listening to it. Among all these people there were many who indeed understood the lofty words, but a larger number who were not up to subtle examination of his thought: uncultivated men, artisans engaged in menial occupations, womenfolk untrained in such learning, a group of children, older people past their prime. All these need the sort of discourse that, through a gentle persuasion of their souls, leads them, through the visible world and the beautiful things in it, to a knowledge of him who made everything.[16] So if one judges what is said against the objective of the great man's teaching, there is nothing missing from the words. For he did not embark on a polemical discourse, weaving it together in a passionate way in order to counter the objections thrown up by others'[17] research, but rather his discourse was more by way of a simple commentary on the text. His aim was to make his discourse more suitable to the simplicity of his hearers,

16. See *hom* 1.7, "... the world is a work of art, set before all for contemplation, so that through it the wisdom of Him who created it should be known ..."; and 1.11, "... and from the greatness of these perceptible and circumscribed bodies let us conceive of Him who is infinite and immense and who surpasses all understanding in the plenitude of His power."

17. "Others'" is not in the Greek.

while at the same time to provide a commentary on it for his more sophisticated listeners which somehow rose with them to a higher level and represented the complex conclusions of philosophy as practiced outside the church.[18] [D11]. Thus it would be understood by the many but admired by the learned.

5. Suppose that,[19] as on Mount Sinai, you had left the multitude of the people down below and had been raised up above everyone else in understanding. Suppose you were aspiring to go with the great Moses into the darkness where things that cannot be spoken of can be contemplated, in which, when he was there, he saw what cannot be seen and heard what cannot be spoken. Suppose you wanted to know what the necessary order of creation was, why after the heaven and earth had come into being, the light awaited the divine command "Let there be light," while the darkness existed without any command.[20] And if light needed nothing else in order for it to illuminate the air that lay below it and to separate the period of the night from that of the day, why was the creation of the sun needed?[21] And if in the begin-

18. Literally, "of the philosophy outside," τῆς ἔξω φιλοσοφίας.

19. Literally, "if" (also in later sentences in this section beginning with "Suppose"). There is no apodosis corresponding to these protases until "Then I would advise . . ." at the end of the section. See Risch, 118, n. 51.

20. In §§10 and 13, Gregory implies that darkness is the absence of light and was dissipated only when fire first emerged from the initial mixture of elements where its brightness had been obscured by earth. Basil's account (2.4–5) is not all that different. Neither author gives any sort of metaphysical or theological explanation of the origin of darkness; see Costache, "Making Sense," 15–17.

21. This is a different formulation of the question raised in §3; see n. 12.

ning the earth came into being with the heaven, why was what came into being "unformed"?[22] For there seems to be no difference in meaning between "to form" and "to make."[23] So if making is the same thing as forming, how can what is made be unformed?[24] And [D12] there is the doubt raised about the wet substance:[25] it would not be possible for something fluid to take a spherical form and to sit above the vault of heaven. For how could what is liquid be set upon the convexity, when what is wet must absolutely necessarily flow down from what is always at the top of the sphere to the sloping part of the shape? How, when that which lies below it is never at rest,[26] can it have any stability when its support is always slipping away? How could what was sitting on top of the pole not be dissipated, as the latter's rapid rotation squirted it away? Moreover, to critics the exhaustibility of the wet nature[27] seems unlikely, since accumulations of water in streams and rivers and seas and pools always [M68] seem to be the same in volume, except when streams which are full

22. ἀκατασκεύαστον, as in the LXX version of Gn 1.2; literally, "unequipped," but it could also be translated as "unprepared" or "unfinished" or "not manufactured." See Liddell & Scott and Lampe, s.v. Perhaps "in a raw state" would be an acceptable paraphrase.

23. τὸ κατασκευάσαι and τὸ ποιῆσαι.

24. In §16, Gregory deals with this issue by differentiating between the initial creation and when the earth had "become solid by virtue of its corporeal qualities."

25. A periphrasis for "water." Basil (*hom* 3.5–9) believed that the water above the firmament was real, physical water. In this section Gregory anticipates his later argument (§§28–63) that Basil is wrong about that, and that the water above the firmament was purely "intelligible" (spiritual).

26. τοῦ ὑποκειμένου ἀστατοῦντος: i.e., the rotating sphere of heaven.

27. Another periphrasis for "water," which Gregory uses throughout *hex.*

to the brim with water overflow because rain or snow has seeped into them, like a mountain torrent which dries up or increases in accordance with the precipitation from above. When the stream flows constantly without decreasing or increasing in volume, all agree that it must follow that the wet substance is not used up; for what is consumed away cannot remain in a constant quantity. Nor would fire, if it really consumes water, remain in a constant quantity, not increased and not fed; for it is not possible for the nature of the fire not to increase at the same time as the material[28] is consumed away. Suppose you are inquisitive about these matters and those like them, and, straining forward towards everything on high [D13], want yourself to see even those things which were exposed to Moses's vision in the cloud and to bring them before the eyes of the many. Then I would advise Your Sagacity[29] to look towards nothing else than the grace that is in you and to investigate the divine depths through the spirit of revelation[30] which has appeared to you through your prayers.

6. Since according to the law laid down by the Apostle we should be slaves to each other in love[31] and it is appropriate to the slavery he commends that we should put each other's commands into effect, I shall try, as best I can, briefly to disclose my opinions, using your prayers as

28. That is, the water. Basil (3.5) believed that there was need for a spare supply of physical water above the firmament to "top up" the water below the firmament, which was being consumed by fire. Gregory deals with that at length in §§28–63.

29. τῇ φρονήσει σου: a term of respectful address to his bishop brother; see Risch, 122, n. 70, and Lampe, s.v., 3.

30. See 1 Cor 2.10.

31. See Gal 5.13.

my ally in my argument. But before I embark on this, let it be solemnly affirmed that we do not contest any of the views of the holy Basil in his philosophical account of the origin of the world, even when, by virtue of the principle of sequential order,[32] the argument leads to an alternative interpretation. Let those views prevail, taking second place only to the inspired Old Testament. Let our views, on the other hand, be set before our readers as exercises undertaken speculatively, and let no harm be caused to anyone by them if anything contrary to the common understanding is found in them.[33] We are not setting out dogma in what we say, which would provide an opportunity to those who revile us. Rather, we are undertaking [D14] only to exercise our own reasoning upon existing opinions, not to lay down exegetical teaching for our successors. Let no one demand that my text should involve itself with the objections that have been leveled against us from Holy Scripture or from what has been explained to us directly by our teacher[34] but does not seem to be consistent with common understanding. It is not my intention to think up a defense for what on the face of it appear to be contradictions. But may I be allowed to examine, so far as I am able, the meanings of texts on the

32. ἔκ τινος ἀκολουθίας: see n. 57.

33. Gregory's claim to be a "research theologian," rather than a dogmatist, is reminiscent of Origen. See Köckert, 405, and compare Henri Crouzel, *Origen,* trans. from the French by A. S. Worrall (Edinburgh: T. & T. Clark, 1998), 163–69.

34. I follow Forbes's text, which reads ἐκ τῶν παραπόδας παρὰ τοῦ διδασκάλου ἡμῶν ἑρμηνευθέντων; the mss. mostly have παραπόδας or παρὰ πόδας. This ought to mean "immediately"; hence my translation "directly." PG and Drobner have the conjectural περὶ πόδα, but I do not see that that makes any more sense; Liddell & Scott (s.v. πούς, 6c) say that it means "fitting exactly (like a shoe)."

basis of what their particular intention is, with a view to the possibility of, with the help of God, working out a coherent and sequentially ordered theory of the creation of things, while retaining the proper significance of the words of the text.[35]

---

7. "In the beginning," it says, "God made the heaven and the earth," and then goes on to what follows, what is said about the origin of the world, that is, the things that came into being in the six days.[36] But before investigating the text, I think it is necessary, for the purposes of my account, [M69] to agree that in the divine nature will and power go together and that God's will is the measure of his power. His will is wisdom. It is the property of wisdom not to be ignorant of how any individual thing can come to be. His power is united with his knowledge, so that it knows what needs to come into being; the [D15] power to create beings goes along with it and brings to actuality what has been conceived in thought. The power does not act after the knowledge; the action is manifested in conjunction with the will, without any separation between the two. For the power is at the same time the will; it considers in advance[37] how beings can come into

35. This is the end of the introduction to *hex,* the first of the six parts into which it can conveniently be divided; see introduction, part 5, pp. 12–13. The second (§§7–11) gives an overview of the philosophical and theological principles that underlie Gregory's interpretation of the Genesis account of the creation, referring to Gn 1.1–2.

36. Drobner's text is … καὶ τὰ ἐφεξῆς, ὅσα περιέχει τῆς κοσμογενίας ὁ λόγος. τὰ μὲν δὴ γεγενημένα κατὰ τὴν ἑξαήμερον ταῦτα, χρὴ δέ, οἶμαι, πρὸ τῆς ἐξετάσεως … I follow the PG text and Forbes, which have a comma after ὁ λόγος, and start a new sentence with Χρὴ δέ. The overall sense is the same, I believe, whichever punctuation is adopted.

37. προβουλεύουσα. As Risch (127, n. 88) observes, this is not, strictly

existence and provides the starting point for the actual existence[38] of what had been thought of, so that, with regard to the creation, one can think at the same time about everything that is of God—his will, his wisdom, his power, and the being of what is.[39] That being so, let no one who undertakes research into matter, investigating how and from where it came into being, let themselves be pushed into a corner. People can indeed be heard saying things like,[40] "If God is immaterial, where does matter come from? How can quantity come from what has no quantity, what is visible from what is invisible, what is obviously circumscribed in mass and dimension from what has neither size nor boundary? How and from where can he who has none of these in his own nature bring forth all the other characteristics that can be observed in matter?" Each of the difficulties that can be raised about matter has, in our view, a single solution. The wisdom of God cannot be held to be powerless; neither can his power be without wisdom. These attributes rather go together, so that both appear as one thing, so that each is seen with the other at one and the same time. For his wise will is manifested in the potentiality of what is actualized, and his active power is perfected in his wise will.[41] So if [D16]

---

speaking, consistent with what Gregory has just said, that the power does not act after the knowledge.

38. "Actual existence" = τὴν ὕπαρξιν.

39. For a discussion of the apparent identification of God's will and the created universe in this passage and elsewhere, see introduction, part 5.1, pp. 14–16.

40. οἷα δὴ λεγόντων ἐστὶν ἀκούειν. I follow PG and Forbes in reading a semicolon before this phrase in the Greek (rendered by a full stop in my translation); Drobner has a comma.

41. Both "potentiality" and "power" in this sentence translate δύναμις; see n. 6 and introduction, part 5.1, pp. 14–15.

his wisdom and power are united and the same, he is not ignorant about how matter can be found for the formation of beings, nor is he too weak to bring into actuality what he has conceived in thought. In order to produce beings, he who can do everything put together, by his wise and powerful will, everything through which matter subsists: lightness, heaviness, compactness, looseness, softness, hardness, wetness, dryness, coldness, heat, color, shape, boundary,[42] spacing;[43] in themselves all these are bare notions and concepts. Nothing of these things is in itself matter; rather, matter is produced when they come together with each other.[44]

8. So if through the superiority of God's wisdom and his power he knows everything and can do everything, perhaps we can get close to the sublime voice of Moses, who says that "in summary" (this is how [D17] Aquila translates, rather than "in the beginning")[45] the heaven and the earth were made by God. The prophet produced the book of Genesis as an introduction to the knowledge

42. Drobner reads ἐπιγραφήν, as, it appears, does Risch, who translates as "die Umschreibung." PG and Forbes read περιγραφὴν, which is found in some mss. I follow PG; Liddell & Scott and Lampe both say that ἐπιγραφή means "inscription," "title," or "description," none of which seems to make sense in this context.

43. διάστημα. See n. 36 in the introduction for a discussion of this concept.

44. So Gregory seems to be rejecting the idea of there being a formless substrate (ὑποκείμενον) on which form is later imposed, as found in Plato's *Timaeus* and later Platonists, and to be denying that "matter," as a distinct concept, is a precondition for the corporeal world. See the discussion in the introduction, part 5.1, pp. 17–20.

45. Aquila was a Jewish proselyte who translated the Hebrew Bible into Greek in the second century CE (see also n. 100 below). He rendered the Hebrew of Gn 1.1 as ἐν κεφαλαίῳ, "in summary," rather than ἐν ἀρχῇ, "in the beginning," the LXX translation.

of God;[46] Moses's aim was to lead those who are enslaved to sense-impressions through what can be perceived to what lies beyond the apprehension of the senses. What we can know by sight is confined to heaven and earth. So the text names, as comprehending what exists, the things that lie at the limit of what can be known by our senses. By saying that these confining bounds came into being through God, it includes everything that is contained within those extremes.[47] [M72] Instead of saying that God made "everything all at once,"[48] it says that "in summary" or "in the beginning," God made the heaven and the earth. The meaning of the two words "beginning" and "summary" is the same, since both equally indicate "everything all at once";[49] for in the word "summary" there is the connotation of everything coming into being collectively, while instantaneity and absence of spacing are evoked by the "beginning." For "beginning" is alien from any idea of spacing; as a point is the beginning of a line, and the atom the beginning of mass, so is what is instantaneous the beginning of temporal spacing.[50]

[D18] 9. So the simultaneous[51] laying of the foundations[52] of what exists, through the indescribable power of God, is called by Moses either "beginning" or "summary";

46. Gregory attributes a similar objective to Basil; see §4 and n. 16 above.

47. So for Gregory the Genesis 1 account has nothing to say about the creation of the invisible world (angels), as is made clear in §14.

48. ἀθρόως; the word carries a connotation of "crowded together in a mass."

49. τὸ ἀθρόον; see previous note.

50. For this notion of an initial simultaneous creation, see introduction, part 5.2, pp. 20–22.

51. ἀθρόα.

52. "Laying of the foundations" = καταβολή.

it is from that origin that everything is said to have been composed. He speaks of the limits of what exists, and at the same time tacitly refers to what lies between those limits; I say "limits" with reference to human sense-perception, which can neither penetrate to what lies under the earth nor pass through heaven. So what this "beginning" of the coming into being of the universe invites us to think is that God laid down the starting points, the causes, and the potentialities[53] of everything that exists collectively and instantaneously, and that in the initial impulse of his will the being of each thing that is came together concurrently: heaven, ether,[54] stars, fire, air, sea, earth, animals, and plants. Everything is seen by the eye of God and is made manifest under the aspect of his power;[55] as the prophecy says, "He knows everything before it comes into being."[56] His power and wisdom are laid down as foundations, and a certain necessary order follows on, according to a certain sequence,[57] with a view to bringing to completion each part of the world. One particular thing,[58] therefore, [D19] of those things that can be seen in the universe, comes first and appears first, and so what necessarily follows after what comes first, and then the third, as nature the artificer requires;[59] then the fourth

53. δυνάμεις. Elsewhere in this section δύναμις means "[God's] power," and I so translate it. See n. 6 and Risch, 126, n. 85.

54. The fiery upper part of the atmosphere.

55. τῷ τῆς δυνάμεως λόγῳ. See n. 53.

56. Dn 13.42 (Susanna 42).

57. Here translating τάξιν. As Köckert (440) points out, Gregory uses the words ἀκολουθία ("sequence"), εἱρμός ("order"), and τάξις ("arrangement") in more or less the same sense.

58. Light or fire, as will be explained later.

59. ὡς ἡ τεχνικὴ συνηνάγκαζε φύσις. But nature is an artificer only in a secondary sense, because God's wisdom and power are immanent in

and the fifth and the rest according to a sequence, one following on from another. These do not appear as they do by spontaneous chance, through some unordered or accidental process. Each thing came to be, [Moses] says, just as the necessary order of nature requires a sequence among things as they come to be; he uses the form of a narrative to give a philosophical account of theories of natural science,[60] and sets out certain words of command from God as a preliminary to each thing that comes into being. He is acting rightly and piously when he does this. For everything that comes into being according to order and wisdom is an individual direct utterance by God. This is because we do not know what God's nature is; but if we get into our minds his absolute wisdom and his absolute power, we believe we have formed a mental concept of God.[61]

[D20] 10. For this reason, when the totality of things[62] came into being, before anything that formed part of that totality came into view, darkness submerged everything. The brightness of fire, hidden in the constituent parts of matter, had not yet appeared. It was like when pebbles remain invisible in the darkness; they have by nature within themselves the power to cause light, by colliding with each other and producing fire; so when a spark appears from them, they too appear visible because of that illumination. In the same way, all things were invis-

---

it. See the discussion of this and other passages in the introduction, part 5.3, pp. 28–29.

60. περὶ τῶν φυσικῶν δογμάτων φιλοσοφήσας, "having philosophized about theories of nature."

61. Literally, "we believe we have taken God up with our thinking" (τῇ διανοίᾳ).

62. Literally, "the whole" (τὸ ὅλον).

ible and obscure until the nature that causes light came forth into visibility. Everything had just come into being without any differentiation, all at once in a single decisive action[63] of the divine will, [M73] with all the elements jumbled up together;[64] fire was dispersed everywhere, but was darkened by the superior power of the matter, which obscured it. But since its power is something keen and active, once an initial signal for the creation of the world was given to the nature of things by God, it leapt out in advance of everything of a heavier nature, and all things were immediately illuminated by light. What came into being by the power of the Creator, as an expression of wisdom, was explained by Moses as an imperative expression[65] of God [D21]: "God said, Let there be light, and there was light." For, in our opinion at least, with God, word or reason is work. So everything that comes into being comes into being through that word or reason,[66] and nothing irrational, fortuitous, or spontaneous can be imagined in what has its origin in God. One must believe rather that in everything that exists there is also a wise and creative reason, even if it is beyond our range of vision.

63. "Decisive action" = ῥοπῇ.

64. For the "jumbling up of the elements" see the discussion of the passage in part 5.2 of the introduction, pp. 23–25.

65. The various words that Gregory uses for "word," "voice," "expression," or "utterance" do not in general have one-to-one equivalents in English, which presents a challenge to the translator. λόγος in particular is notoriously tricky. Here and earlier in this sentence I render it "expression." But in the next sentence and later, I translate it as "word" or "reason" and later occasionally as "principle" or "rational principle." In *hex* it never explicitly refers to the Second Person of the Trinity; see introduction, part 5.1, pp. 16–17.

66. λόγῳ: see previous note.

11. So since the expression[67] "God said" suggests word or reason, the pious way, in my view, for us to think about it is for us to apply that utterance to the word or reason that lies within creation. For the great David also explained such expressions to us in a similar way, when he said, "In wisdom you have made everything."[68] For the utterance that commanded the creation of what exists, recorded by Moses as an expression of God, is what David called the wisdom that can be seen in what has come into being. Hence he also says that the heavens declare the glory of God,[69] clearly because, for those who understand, God's artistic vision, which is revealed through the heavens' harmonious revolutions, fulfills the same role as his creative word.[70] When he says that the heavens declare and the firmament [D22] proclaims, he corrects those who take that expression in a crude sense and perhaps expect the sound of a voice and an articulated utterance from the declaration of the heavens; he says, "There are no utterances or words, nor are their voices heard."[71] This is so that he can show that the wisdom that is seen in creation is "word," even if not articulated. Later, too, Moses says that detailed utterances were made to him by God during the wonderful signs produced in Egypt. The psalmist interprets these in a more elevated way than could be popularly comprehended when he says, "He es-

67. Here and in the next sentence, "expression" translates φωνή, and "word or reason" translates λόγος.

68. Ps 103 (104).24.

69. Ps 18 (19).1.

70. Literally: "Clearly, for those who understand, the craftsman-like vision (τῆς … τεχνικῆς θεωρίας), which is revealed through the harmonious revolutions, is instead of a word" (λόγου).

71. Ps 18 (19).3.

tablished among them the words of his signs and wonders in the land of Ham."[72] By this expression the psalmist clearly alludes to the fact that it is by word or reason that the potentiality that is in everything is brought into actuality. The "word" is not expressed in what is said, but is so called because of its power to produce signs.[73]

---

12. So it was, then, that the power of light emerged and, in the swiftness and mobility of its nature, was separated from what is.[74] It separated itself from things of a different nature, and everything on which its beams fell was brought into light through its radiant power. According to what principle the substance of fire[75] can achieve this, only God, who placed the rational principle of light[76] in its nature, can say. The great Moses, [M76] too, testifies to this in his own text, when he says, "And God said, Let there be light."[77] I think that through what he says here he is teaching that it is the divine word [D23], transcending every human concept, that causes light to work.[78] For we look only at what has come into existence, and appreciate the wonder through our senses. Where

72. Ps 104 (105).27. "The words" (τοὺς λόγους) is in the LXX text but not found in modern translations.

73. This is the end of the second part of *hex,* largely devoted to setting out general principles. The third part (§§12–26) gives a more detailed interpretation of Genesis 1.1–10.

74. For the notion of creation as a progressive separation from an original undifferentiated mass—"Diakrisis-Kosmogonie"—see part 5.3 of the introduction, p. 29.

75. Gregory regards light as a property of fire, to bring it into the framework of the four traditional elements: earth, air, fire, and water.

76. Literally, "the light-giving λόγος."

77. Gn 1.3.

78. Literally, "that is the work of light."

fire has latently been[79] before it is suddenly generated, whether it springs up from pebbles colliding with each other, or from some other kind of things rubbing together, and what the power is that consumes whatever it seizes on and illuminates the air with its flame, we can neither see nor form any conception of. We say rather that it is only in God that the word or reason behind this amazing wonder is to be found. It is he who made light be engendered in fire, according to the unspoken word or reason of his power, as Moses testifies in his own words when he says, "And God said, Let there be light, and there was light, and God saw the light, that it was beautiful and good."[80] It is truly only God who could see how what was "beautiful and good" in this way could come to be. The poverty of our nature sees what has come to be, but is incapable of either seeing or praising the rational principle according to which it came to be. For praise is appropriate only to what is known, not to what is unknown.

13. So, he says, God saw the light, that it was beautiful and good, and God made a division between the light on one side and the darkness on the other. Again Moses refers to the action of God what happens necessarily, in accordance with the sequence of nature, in a certain order and harmony. [D24] Through his words he is teaching, I think, that everything that comes forth in some necessary order according to the principle of sequence has been

79. Literally, "where the fire is living" (διαιτώμενον).

80. "Beautiful and good" = καλὸν. Our familiar modern translations of Gn 1.4 and subsequent corresponding verses have just "good." But the Greek word connotes both beauty and goodness, and to translate it as just "good" would be misleading in some contexts. See, for example, §31 below.

perceived in advance by the wisdom of God. The substance of light, dispersed everywhere, was combined with what was of the same kind and all concentrated together.[81] What was necessarily obscured by the matter of the other elements[82] was overshadowed, and the overshadowing was darkness. This happened according to the principle of sequence, but so that nobody should attribute it to some random chance, Moses says that it was a work of God; it was a potentiality that had been built into what had come into existence.

14. But it is clear to everybody from what is visible to us[83] that the nature of fire is keen and tending upward and ever-moving. What is represented to the mind as a consequence of that starting-point is recorded by Moses as history, in the form of a narrative, when he also writes, "And there was evening, and there was morning."[84] For who does not realize that, since creation is conceived of as divided into two, the intellectual and the sensible, the whole concern here of the lawgiver[85] is not to explain the intellectual creation, but, using things that are visible to us, to demonstrate the orderly arrangement of sensible things? When all things were constituted,[86] fire, [D25]

81. Literally, "was all concentrated (ἀθροισθείσης) around itself."

82. Literally, "by what was left (τῇ λοιπῇ) of the matter of the elements."

83. "To us" is not in the Greek.

84. Gn 1.5.

85. Moses.

86. Literally, "Since (ἐπεὶ), when all things were constituted …" In the Greek, the main clause to which that is subordinate seems to be what I have translated below as a separate sentence, beginning, "For this reason" (τούτου χάριν). I therefore think it is better to have a semicolon in the Greek text before τούτου χάριν (Forbes and PG) than a full stop (Drobner).

alien from everything evil.[110] There is a myriad of texts from Holy Scripture that can be produced about this, to the effect that God is the true light and that he dwells in unapproachable light. But the Spirit of God is by nature the same as God himself.[111] If God and the Spirit are of one nature, and God is light, the Spirit of God too must be entirely light. But light necessarily makes light those things to which it is brought.[112] So the water, to which the Spirit of God was brought, was completely in the light and was separated from the darkness. But what was not in darkness had absolutely no need of light.[D32] If we think about the probabilities here, the water to which the light was brought is different from the downward-tending nature of the waters that flow here;[113] it is walled off by the firmament from the heavy and downward-tending water. Let nobody be surprised by the use of the same word, if that which, according to our theory, means, according to a more lofty interpretation, the plenitude of intellectual powers[114] is also called "water" by the Scripture. For, in a similar way, God is a "consuming fire,"[115] but the expression is free of the material connotations of fire. So you have learned that God is a fire, but you think of him

110. On the link between darkness and evil, see introduction, part 6.2, n. 83.

111. As Gregory argues forcefully in his three books against Eunomius, rebutting the views of the "Pneumatomachoi" ("Spirit-fighters") or "Macedonians."

112. οἷς ἐπιφέρεται: see n. 108 above.

113. Here and in the following four sections Gregory challenges Basil's theory of water. In the next part of his work, he will set out at length more detailed scientific arguments in defense of his view. See introduction, part 6.2, pp. 32–36.

114. That is, presumably, the angels and the powers of heaven described in Col 1.16.

115. Dt 4.24.

having been shot out like an arrow from the elements of a different nature, leapt out first from everything else, because the motion that it has by nature is light and tends upward. But it was not able, as it passed through sensible being like a thought, to direct its motion into a straight line; the intellectual creation cannot be mixed with sensible things on a common basis, and fire is one of those sensible things. For this reason, [M77] when fire reached the outer limits of creation, it necessarily adopted a circular motion.[87] It is compelled by the power which lies within its nature to be carried along in all directions, but as it has no room to continue its course in a straight line—for all the sensible world is confined by its own boundaries—it travels along the extreme limits of sensible nature, where it can move freely; as we have said before, intellectual nature would not allow fire to move along within itself. It is for this reason that Moses, following the movement of fire in his thought, said that when light emerged it did not stay in its original place but surrounded the grosser substance of other existing things[88] and in its furious motion brought in turn, through its revolution, light to what was not illuminated and darkness to what was illuminated.

15. This succession according to regular temporal intervals—I mean light and darkness—having arisen across the region below [D26], Moses again attributed to God the giving of the names "day" and "night." He did not admit the thought that anything that had arisen from the

87. Gregory here departs from Aristotle, who says that the circular movement originated with the (ethereal) stellar sphere. See Risch, 167–69, n. 165, and Köckert, 449.

88. "Other" is not in the Greek.

principle of sequential order should have an origin that was spontaneous or located in something else. This is why he said, "God called the light day, and the darkness he called night."[89] The power of light cannot, by its nature, stand still, so that when light had passed through the upper part of the circuit and took its way towards what lay below, what now[90] lay above the fire was necessarily cast into shadow when the fire took its course below it; as was to be expected, the more solid nature obscured the brightness. So the going down of the light he called "evening"; and again, when the fire had finished the part of its circuit that lay below the earth and brought its brightness to what lay above, he called this event "morning," which was the name he gave to the dawn.

16. But let us return briefly to what we have said already, so that what has been supplied by Holy Scripture and demonstrates the coherence of the theory[91] that has been handed down to us may give us its support. The account of the origin of the world says at the outset, "In the beginning God made the heaven and the earth."[92] We interpret this as follows: that the account is presenting us with the origin of beings all together at the same time [D27], indicating both the external boundaries and what lies between them. For what is in the middle is completely included within the outer limits. The outer limits are, so far as human sense-perception is concerned, heaven and earth, since human vision is limited by these on

89. Gn 1.5.

90. "Now" is not in the Greek.

91. Literally, "what has been supplied (τὰ παρεθέντα) by Holy Scripture towards the sequence (πρὸς τὸν εἱρμὸν) of the theory ..."

92. Gn 1.1.

both sides. He who said, "The limits of the earth are in his hands"[93] included within the compass of those limits what was in the middle. Moses too, in the same way, described the laying of the foundations of the material part of the whole world by referring to its limits. We say that the words that come in between[94] support this notion: it is written, "For the earth was invisible and unformed."[95] It is clear from this that in God's first impulse towards creation everything potentially existed. It was as if some seminal power[96] to make things come into existence had been sown but there were not yet any individual beings in actuality. "The earth," he says, "was invisible and unformed," which [M80] is equivalent to saying that it both existed and did not exist; for there were not yet any qualities associated with it.[97] The proof of this view is that the text says the earth was invisible [D28]. What can be seen is color; color is a sort of emanation of the shape as it appears to the sight;[98] and there can be no shape without a body. So if the earth was invisible, it was altogether without color; being without color, it must be thought of as without shape; without shape, it must be considered as without a body. So in the simultaneous laying of the foundations of the world, the earth was included in the things that are—as indeed was everything else. But it awaited

93. Ps 94 (95).4.

94. That is, Gn 1.2, now to be quoted, which comes between Gn 1.1 and 1.3–5, verses Gregory has already discussed.

95. Gn 1.2.

96. Οἱονεὶ σπερματικῆς τινος δυνάμεως. The word καταβολή, translated as "laying of the foundations," can also mean "sowing," which suits the simile. For the idea of a cosmogenic "seed," found in several ancient philosophers, see introduction, n. 46.

97. Literally, "For the qualities had not yet assembled around it."

98. Literally, "of the shape according to its appearance."

the effect of the provision of qualities; that is what constitutes actually coming into existence.[99] So when the account says the earth was "invisible," it is showing that no other quality was to be observed in it; and when it calls it "unformed," it is inviting us to think that it had not yet become solid by virtue of its corporeal qualities.

17. This idea is explained more clearly in the translations by Symmachus, Theodotion, and Aquila.[100] The first says, "The earth was undeveloped and indistinct"; the second,[101] "emptiness and nothing"; the third, "thing and nothing."[102] In my view at any rate, what is shown by these terms is, by "undeveloped," that in actuality the earth did not actually exist but possessed existence only potentially, and, by [D29] "indistinct," that each of its qualities was not yet separated from the others and could not be individually recognized. Instead, the totality was perceived in a confused and indistinct quality; neither color nor shape nor bulk nor weight nor size nor anything else of that kind could be observed as it was in itself, according to its own rational principle, within the substrate.[103] "Emptiness" and "nothing" too demonstrate the same idea to us. By the word "emptiness" he indicated to us the potential to produce qualities, so that through this we might learn that the Creator of all laid down in advance a potentiality

99. Literally, "which is coming into existence" (γενέσθαι).

100. Second-century (probably) translators into Greek of the Hebrew Scriptures, all of whose versions were included in Origen's *Hexapla*. See *ODCC* s.vv.

101. But this in fact seems to be Aquila's rather than Theodotion's translation; see Risch, 175, n. 183.

102. Θὲν (a nonce-word formed from οὐθέν?) καὶ οὐθέν.

103. ἐν τῷ ὑποκειμένῳ This is not a material substrate, but rather the potential existence of individual qualities. See introduction, part 5.2, pp. 20–25.

that was able to take on qualities. This potentiality was "empty" and had "nothing" in it until it was made complete by the qualities. The third expression, being a term devised in the philosophy of Epicurus, should, I think, be left without further consideration. For he says something similar, emptily expressed and worth nothing, about the initial origin of what exists; in using such expressions he shows that the nature of atoms is insubstantial, which is like "thing and nothing."[104]

[D30] 18. But let us return to taking forward our speculation in its proper order, and consider how, when once fire had encircled the outer limits of sensible nature, the firmament which Moses says is between the upper and lower waters came, in sequence, into existence.[105] I think that the firmament should not be conceived as a solid and hard body, whether formed of the four elements or of something other than those, as pagan philosophy imagines. Rather, according to what Scripture says, the firmament is the summit of sensible being, around which the nature of fire revolves by virtue of its power of perpet-

104. Gregory seems to imply that "thing and nothing" is a term derived from Epicurus's philosophy. This might allude to the latter's doctrine that nothing can come from nothing and that the universe has always existed. But perhaps more likely, in the light of what comes next, is that it refers to his notion that atoms ("thing") and empty space ("nothing") are the basic building blocks of the universe. "Emptily [or carelessly] expressed and worth nothing" (κενοφώνον δὲ καὶ μηδέν), as well as being deliberately rude to Epicurus, may be a punning reference to that concept of "emptiness" (see Risch, 176, n. 189). Gregory seems to be arguing, on the basis of the notion that according to Epicurus the nature of atoms was insubstantial (ἀνυπόστατον), that he believed that in one sense atoms both existed and didn't exist ("thing" and "nothing"), although I have not been able to find any evidence that Epicurus in fact believed that.

105. For Gregory's account of the firmament, see introduction, part 6.2, pp. 34–35.

ual motion, and it is contrasted with the characteristics of the eternal, the incorporeal, and the intangible. For who does not know that everything firm is closely compacted together, by virtue of something altogether hard and resistant in its nature? What is dense and hard cannot be free of the quality of weight, while what has weight cannot, by its nature, tend upward. The firmament is situated above the entire sensible creation, but it does not [M81] follow from the logic of the argument that it is thick and corporeal. Rather, as has been said above, everything of the sensible kind is called firm in comparison with what is intellectual and incorporeal, even though by virtue of the subtlety of its nature it may elude our [D31] observation. So whatever is bounded by the revolution of the fire (for what is so bounded is the extreme limit of material nature), what is ultimately and finally[106] circumscribed by its own border, is called the firmament, because of its material nature compared with what lies above. But it has the name of "heaven," as the name "day" was given to the light, and "night" to the darkness.

19. The separation of the waters by the firmament that lies between them is not inconsistent with this theory and follows from Scripture. For after what is said about the earth,[107] it is written in the passage coming next that "darkness was over the deep, and the Spirit of God was brought[108] above the water."[109] Our theory is that the Spirit of God is just as far from being dark as it is

106. "Ultimately and finally" translates ἅπαξ.

107. That is, that it was unformed and invisible (Gn 1.2a).

108. ἐπεφέρετο ἐπάνω, the Septuagint text; "swept across" in modern translations from the Hebrew.

109. Gn 1.2.

as different from the fire that we know;[116] in the same way, you have been taught that water was brought under the divine Spirit, but do not think of it as having the downward-tending nature of the water that flows down into the earth. For the Spirit of God is not brought to lowly and unstable things.

20. So, to reveal our thinking more clearly, we shall repeat the sense of what we have said in a concise form: the firmament, which is called heaven, is the boundary of the sensible creation. Beyond it comes the intellectual creation, in which there is neither form nor size nor spatial location nor measure of spacing nor color nor shape nor magnitude nor any other of those things that can be observed below heaven.

[D33] 21. And let nobody suspect that I am introducing confusion into the way the text should be viewed by using allegory,[117] in line with the conjectures of those who have considered these matters before us and say that "the deep" means the powers who rebelled and that the "darkness over the deep" means the ruler of the world of darkness. May I never transgress so far as to think that evil is a creature of God, given that, summing up, the divine word says clearly that "God saw all that he had made, and, [M84] behold, it was all very beautiful and good"![118] If everything that God made is beautiful and good, and if "the deep" and everything associated with it are not excluded from what was made by God, then those things too are beautiful and good in their own way—even "the

116. Literally, "this fire."

117. For Gregory and Basil on allegory, see part 3, n. 14, of the introduction.

118. Gn 1.31.

deep," and even when the light which falls on all beings does not yet shine on it. When I hear from Scripture of "the deep," I say it means the mass of the waters. That is how the Psalms define it when they say, "The depths were troubled, there was an abundant sound of waters."[119] When I hear of darkness on the depths, my understanding is that the illuminating power found in the nature of things that exist has not yet appeared. I learn from Scripture of the separation of the waters,[120] which came to be through the firmament; I do not think I am going beyond what is probable or the meaning of the words in understanding this in terms of the separation of the water.[121] I think that the nature of each is different. I believe that the one [D34] is upward-tending and light, more imponderable even than the lightness of fire,[122] so that it remains above the warm substance[123] and is neither displaced by the movement of what lies below it nor restored by warmth to its opposing state,[124] but rather

119. Ps 76 (77).16–17 (LXX).

120. N.B. plural. See next note.

121. N.B. singular; see previous note. Risch (189–90, n. 213) suggests that Gregory takes the separation of "the waters" as implying simply the division of a homogeneous body of water into two. But by describing it as the separation of "the water" he indicates a division of the water into two different natures.

122. "Light," "upward-tending," and "imponderable" are slightly odd expressions to use here, to the extent that they seem to imply something material, albeit very subtle and refined; later in the sentence, as elsewhere, Gregory makes it clear that the water above the firmament is immaterial (ἄϋλον).

123. Presumably the fiery ether of the upper air; see §37.

124. That is, brought down into the material, sensible world below the firmament. See Risch (190, n. 214): the warmth of fire can make the (sensible) waters below the firmament move upward, by evaporation, but cannot make the (intellectual) waters above the firmament move downward.

remains undiminished and provides no way through for the fire which moves below it: for how could the immaterial provide a space for the material? The other is our water, whose nature we know by sight and touch and taste. Because of its inherent quality it flows downward, and is seen to be transparent and is recognized by its taste; its nature can be known, and does not require us to interpret it in a transferred sense.[125]

22. So that which is called "water" cannot be seen and does not flow and can in no way be contained by those things by which what is naturally wet can be held under control. Rather, it is beyond any location, unmixed with any quality that can be recognized by the senses. I do not think that any of those who have made a considered judgment do not conceive it as something other than common water, given that it is brought under the Spirit of God, that they believe it is above the heavens, and that it remains beyond anything that is known by the senses. They have been led to the notion of intellectual being by the deeper sense of the words.[126] What we surmise, as a result of our inquiries, is that everything that moves is enclosed within the intellectual nature and turns back around itself. The boundary of things [D35] that move is the edge of spatial nature; beyond it is found intellectual and non-spatial nature, free from local and spatial characteristics.

125. Literally, "to transfer it to some other conception" (ἔννοιαν). The comparison is of course with the "water" above the firmament, which does indeed have to be understood in some sort of "transferred sense."

126. Literally, "being carried to the intellectual being by the deeper senses" (ταῖς ὑπονοίαις).

23. So we say that the furthest edge of sensible nature, beyond which there is nothing of a kind that we recognize by its appearance, is denoted by the word "firmament." Scripture supports our surmise; it says, "God divided in its midst the water that was below the firmament and the water that was above the firmament."[127] Through this it is shown that not even in the beginning was the latter water diluted by the former. Even though they had [M85] the same name, there was no mixing of natures. For what is said is not "that came to be below or above the firmament," but "that was below the firmament and that was above the firmament." If the one, driven down into the lower position, was in darkness from the outset, but the other was not in darkness (because what is in the Spirit of God must necessarily be in the light and separated from darkness) and was also above the firmament which was brought into being between the two, let the wise hearer judge [D36] whether the argument in what we have said fails to lead to a reasonable theory.

24. So this, in general terms,[128] is what we conjecture about the original condition of the things that exist and how, as regards the potentiality for being, light did not come later than those things, even though Scripture records darkness as becoming apparent before light. This is what our theory is about the firmament and the distinction between the waters, whose nature, divided into what

127. Gn 1.7. The LXX text does not refer to "the water that *was* above the firmament" (τοῦ ὕδατος ὃ ἦν ἐπάνω τοῦ στερεώματος) but merely to "the water above the firmament" (τοῦ ὕδατος, τοῦ ἐπάνω τοῦ στερεώματος). Gregory adopts a reading that he believes establishes that the two kinds of water were already distinct before the firmament came into being to separate them.

128. Literally, "these things and such things" (ταῦτα καὶ τὰ τοιαῦτα).

tends downward and what is light in weight, provides us with different concepts for each of the things that bear the same name. The waters, the visible ones and the intellectual ones, were separated from each other, and the heaven was brought forth as the dividing line between the waters of two different natures. It is said to have arisen in the beginning together with the earth and everything that was laid down to construct the universe. Now it is complete and has been given its name, revealed as the firmament,[129] which has as its lower boundary[130] the circulation of fire. So now the second circuit of the light, too,[131] again darkened and illuminated in turn what lay below it; it, too, was called day, as it followed sequentially on the previous one.[132] The nature of number necessarily and sequentially came into existence at the same time as creation. [D37] For all number is a collection of units; the name "unit" is given to everything that we see as circumscribed by a defined boundary. So since the circuit is bounded only by itself on all sides and is complete in itself,[133] it is right that the text should call the one revolution of the cycle by a single name, when it says, "There was evening, and there was morning, one day."[134] In the

129. Gn 1.8: "God called the firmament heaven." Unlike Basil (*hom* 3.3), Gregory identifies the heaven of Gn 1.1 with that in Gn 1.6–8. See n. 13 above.

130. "Lower" is not in the Greek.

131. The first circuit—the first night and day—has been discussed in §§14–15 above. Gregory now reinforces the point that that was the beginning of a continuing cycle of day and night.

132. Literally, "according to the preceding sequence," κατὰ τὴν προλαβοῦσαν ἀκολουθίαν.

133. Literally, "So since on all sides the cycle is lacking nothing, bounded in itself..." Gregory seems to mean that day and night form a complete, autonomous, and indivisible cycle.

134. Gn 1.5.

same way it calls the other circuit[135] "one" as well. He put both together and made two, and so the text introduces the origin of number at the same time as the parts of creation,[136] indicating by the names of the numbers the order of the sequence. For he says, "There was evening, and there was morning, the second day."[137]

25. This being how things happened, the nature of beings, proceeding according to sequence, produced what necessarily follows from what went before. But the divine command preceded this operation too; Moses everywhere established the idea for us that nothing that is comes into existence without God, so that the marvel of everything that comes into being might lead us back to him who made it. The whole of the illuminating and fiery substance was separated from everything else by its characteristic qualities. But nothing is said about the creation of air, although it would have been reasonable to give an account of its nature, too, in the second place, after that of the emergence of fire (since because [D38] of its lightness there is a certain relationship between it and the lightness we observe in fire) and then to discuss the heavy nature. He[138] [M88] talks about the latter, but in his account he passes over air: not because it has no contribution to make to the completeness of the universe as a whole, nor because it does not share in[139] the poten-

135. That is, the second day.

136. I have not discovered whether this interesting idea, that the creation of day and night introduced the concept of duality, and thus of number, multiplicity, and sequence into the created universe, is original to Gregory.

137. Gn 1.8.

138. Moses.

139. Literally, "is separated from."

tiality of the elements,[140] but perhaps because in its soft and pliable nature air is able to receive any existing thing, showing things through itself; it does not have its own color or shape or appearance, but takes its form from the colors and shapes of other things. It becomes bright when it is illuminated by the light and then becomes dark again when it is in shadow. In itself it is neither bright nor dark, but it embraces every shape, is colored by every kind of color, and adapts itself to every motion of the things that move within it. It effortlessly withdraws to either side of what moves, and, divided on this side and that by the weight of the moving object, automatically replaces itself behind. Even when whatever liquid happens to be in an amphora is poured out, it moves aside from what is being poured, and automatically moves in to take over the space that has been left empty. Countless other such things demonstrate that the nature of air is soft and pliable. The [D39] life of human beings is conducted in it, and nearly all the power of life and the activity of the sense-organs get their strength from air; for through it we see and hear and similarly, through inhalation of breath, obtain a perception of things that can be smelled. It is the most important of the things that operate for the purpose of life, because the person who stops breathing assuredly stops living. For this reason Moses in his wisdom left no account of the nature of this element, which is familiar and closely linked to us and in which we are reared right from our birth. He considered that the innate and intimate relationship between our nature and air was an

140. That is, it has just the same potential for developing into the world as we know it as the other elements have.

adequate teacher about this part of cosmogony;[141] in his account he records the creatures that appeared in the air, recounting the individual circumstances of their creation.[142]

26. When the second day had passed, the wise and harmonious ordering of things coming into being which separated the water from the earth was again called the voice and command of God.[143] For everything that happens through wisdom is truly the word of God, not articulated by organs of speech, but expressed through the miraculous quality itself of what comes into view. For the earthly quality was confused together with the wet nature; by who else's power was the earth condensed so as to manifest its characteristic qualities, so that all its parts were squeezed together to combine with what was of a similar nature, and so that in this solidification and [D40] compression the wetness[144] that lay within it was forced out?[145] The water was separated out from its mixture with the earth, and forcibly gathered around itself in the hollow places of the earth. For since these things truly come from the divine power and wisdom, Moses says

141. "Of cosmogony" is not in the Greek.

142. Literally, "... the things that appeared in it according to the creation, how it happened in each case."

143. See Gn 1.9.

144. In this section (and elsewhere) in effect another synonym for "water."

145. All the editions of the Greek text and, apart from Köckert (454), all the translations that I have consulted put a comma or a semi-colon here and the question mark at the end of the following (in my translation) sentence, after "of the earth." As Köckert apparently thinks, I believe it is more plausible syntactically to put the question mark here. In the following sentence Gregory abandons his rhetorical question and reverts to simple exposition.

that the word of God, expressed as an imperative saying, stands at the beginning of this marvel; in my judgment about this, he reveals, through this expressive form of words, the word or reason that lies within the nature of creation. For what he says is, "God said, Let the waters be brought together to their gathering places,[146] [M89] and let the dry land appear."[147] You see the necessary order of nature: how when the water has been drawn away from the earth, that which remains has its wetness drawn out; how when the wetness is no longer mixed with the earth to form mud, the water is necessarily confined to certain receptacles, so that it does not disappear, as it would if nothing contained its spread because of its natural tendency to flow.

---

27. But it does not seem to me to be inappropriate now to make further mention of the waters above the heavens.[148] If, here below, the earth is shaped to contain the waters, as for instance by confining their flow in certain hollow places and, by its own fixity, providing stability to the unstable nature of the waters, how can the

146. εἰς τὰς συναγωγὰς αὐτῶν. LXX has "to one gathering place" (εἰς συναγωγὴν μιὰν) here, although it has "to their gathering places" in the second part of the verse.

147. Gn 1.9.

148. This section is a prelude to the fourth main part of the book—the next thirty-five sections, nearly half of it—which are devoted to explaining why Basil's theory (*hom* 3.5–9), that the (physical) waters above the firmament are created to "top up" those below the firmament, which are constantly being consumed by fire, is unnecessary and false. For a summary of Gregory's argument, see part 6 of the introduction. It is particularly in this part of the book that Gregory draws extensively on the scientific ideas and terminology of his time: see section 4 of the introduction.

water above, [D41] if it really is water, sit stably on what is unstable and remain on a convex surface without flowing away? For if we assume that the two waters have one and the same natures, it is absolutely necessary to think that what we see in one applies also to the other. So the hilly ridges of heaven are divided by valleys, in the same way as those on earth; they are made into gullies, with space between their banks, so that the water may be contained within the hollows! What will people say when the cyclical revolution of the sphere of heaven brings down below what is now above? Will they even imagine some sort of lids on the cycles, so that the water, suspended, will not flow out of the hollow places?[149]

28. But he[150] says that fire is consuming and that there is need for some nourishing sustaining material to keep the flame in permanent existence; otherwise, it would die away through lack of kindling, totally consumed away.[151] But even though the powerful voice of our teacher may agree with such a hypothesis, I beg my readers not to be upset if, having regard to the principle of sequence, I myself do not slavishly follow in every respect those who are pre-eminent in the science of being. For it was not the intention even of our teacher [D42] to prescribe his own theories as laws for his audience but rather

149. Gregory is satirizing Basil's view that the waters above the firmament have the same physical qualities as those below. I do not know precisely what picture he has in mind when he writes of "some sort of lids on the cycles," πώματά τινα τοῖς κύκλοις.

150. "He" is Basil, who says that God knew how much water had to be set aside for "consumption" (δαπάνην) by fire, and that that is the reason for the apparently excessive amount of water in creation (*hom* 3.5, PG 29:65A).

151. Literally, "consumed around itself," αὐτὸ περὶ ἑαυτὸ δαπανώμενον.

that there should be, through his teachings, a way for his disciples to access the truth. So we too, trained in the teachings that he has left to us, have regard to the principle of sequence. But may our argument too, if it turns out to be reasonable, be referred back to the wisdom of our teacher.

29. So what is our argument to be in response to the objections that are raised against us?[152] It is not only in fire and water that we observe opposite qualities; within the characteristics of each of the elements one can also find a kind of conflict with their opposites. As, in the case of the elements we have mentioned, warmth resists cold, and dryness resists wetness, so too there is another diametric opposition in the case of earth and air; in both there are opposing qualities that are set against each other:[153] being compact or being loose, solid or of low density, heavy or light, and whatever else in the characteristics of each of these are recognized as opposites. In these cases it is not possible to say that one thing is fed by its opposite: the lightness of air is not increased by the consumption of what is heavy, nor does the solidity of earth bring about the low density of the opposite element,[154] [D43], nor do the other [M92] characteristics of earth, through consumption of themselves, feed the qualities of the air. In the same way one says that wet and cold are the opposite

152. For the theory set out in this section and the next about opposing qualities and their relationship with the transformation of elements, see part 6.3 of the introduction, pp. 36–37.

153. Literally, "so again, in accordance with the other diametric opposition (κατὰ τὴν ἑτέραν διάμετρον), in the case of earth and air, in both there are qualities set in opposition (ἐξ ἐναντίου … ἀντικαθήμεναι) to each other."

154. τοῦ ἀντιστοιχοῦντος: literally, "what stands opposite to it (as its pair)." Air is clearly meant.

of hot and dry, but not that the one is fed by the destruction of the other, nor that each of these has the potential of existence by virtue of the non-existence of the other. For neither of them would exist if the potential survival of both depended on the destruction of both.[155] For each has the same potential to destroy the other; whenever the predominant one increases, the one that is found wanting disappears.

30. We can discover empirically[156] that this account is true. When fire seizes on some material and water is then put on it, the reciprocal destruction of these two[157] of them can clearly be seen. The predominant one eliminates the other; each yields equally to the sovereignty of whoever wins the upper hand. When the power of both is equal, what is produced is reciprocal elimination of both; it is not that the one is fed by the other, but that the two make each other disappear. In the case of wild animals that eat each other, nature does not provide that those which are destroyed by each other are dependent on each other for life;[158] in the same way, the opposition

155. Literally, "if the continuance (διαμονὴ) of both had its potentiality in the destruction of the two." Perhaps Gregory would have expressed his meaning more clearly if he had said, "if the potential survival of either depended on the destruction of the other."

156. Literally, "from experience itself," ἐξ αὐτῆς ... τῆς πείρας.

157. It seems likely that by "these two" Gregory means the competing qualities of hot and dry and cold and wet, on the lines he discusses in the previous section. But it may be that he is pointing out that in some circumstances one or the other of the elements themselves, fire and water, can make the other one temporarily disappear. See introduction, part 6.3, pp. 36–37.

158. Gregory's use of "animals that eat each other" as an analogy seems rather confusing, in that a carnivorous predator is ultimately dependent on its prey for its life (although the reverse is not of course the case). The point of the analogy is presumably that the *destruction,* that is, the death of the victim, is not in itself necessary for the predator to

of wet and dry would not preserve either [D44] in being if the destruction of one fed the other.

31. But it seems to me that it is right for us to understand the text more in terms of sequence. Since everything that God created is "very beautiful and good,"[159] my view is that we should look for the perfection of beauty and goodness in everything that exists. The addition of "very" clearly shows, through its sense of intensification, that nothing of perfection is absent. When the animals come into being, it is possible to see countless differences between their different kinds. But we say that it is appropriate to apply to each of them the general expression of commendation of all[160] beings, to say that they are equally "very beautiful and good." The commendation does not apply to what they look like. If it did, would "very beautiful and good" apply to the millipede and the toad and the creatures engendered from decaying filth?[161] But the eye of God does not have regard to creatures' blooming beauty, nor does it define beauty and goodness in terms of a fine color or a fine shape, but rather in terms of how each thing, in its being, has in itself a complete and perfect[162] nature. To be

survive. The fact that it then goes on to eat it, and thus sustain itself, is, in this context, irrelevant.

159. Gn 1.31, where "very" is added to "beautiful and good" (on which see n. 80 above).

160. "All" is not in the Greek.

161. I follow Köckert (492, n. 397) in making this sentence an interrogative one. If read as a statement (as in other editions and translations), it is inconsistent with what Gregory says a few lines later, that in the eyes of God at least creepy-crawlies are indeed "beautiful and good." (Galen takes a similarly positive view of them, in opposition to the Aristotelians, who believed that their origin lacked any final cause and that they arose spontaneously and automatically and therefore irrationally. See Köckert, 493 and n. 400.)

162. "Complete and perfect" = τελείαν.

a horse does not mean not being a cow. Rather, in each its nature preserves itself. Its nature has been given its own individual starting point, which enables it to continue to be in its own individual way.[163] It has its own power to exist without requiring the destruction of another nature.[164] So even though the elements are different from each other, each in itself is "very beautiful and good." For in each case, in accordance with its own rational principle, there is [D45] a fulfillment of beauty and goodness. Earth is a "beautiful and good" thing; it does not need the destruction of air in order to be earth, but continues in its own qualities by virtue of the natural power from God that is contained within it and which is able to preserve itself. Air is a "beautiful and good" thing, not because it is not earth, but because, through the powers that it naturally has within it, it has what it needs in order to continue to be. So too water is "very beautiful and good," and fire is "very beautiful and good," each brought to fulfillment in its own individual qualities and able to stay continually in existence by the power of the divine will according to the measure established for it in the original creation. It is said that "the earth stands forever,"[165] without decrease or increase. Air is kept within its own boundaries, fire does not diminish; why, of all these, is it only water that is consumed away?

32. And furthermore [M93] we see how abundant

163. Literally, "having obtained its own individual starting points for the purpose of its own individual continuance."

164. Here I follow Risch's reading (200, n. 255): οὐκ ἐν φθορᾷ τῆς φύσεως ἄλλης τὴν τοῦ εἶναι δύναμιν ἔχουσα. Forbes and Drobner have οὐκ ἐν φθορᾷ τῆς φύσεως, ἀλλ' εἰς τὴν τοῦ εἶναι δύναμιν ἔχουσα. Both have ms. support, and the general sense is more or less the same for either reading.

165. Eccl 1.4.

the nature and power of fire is, compared with other[166] things that exist. It has been clearly shown by those who have made philosophical investigations in astronomy that the sun is many times bigger than the earth, so that the shadow cast by it[167] does not extend to the whole atmosphere; by virtue of the superior size of the sun, as its beams radiate the shadow is restricted to the shape of a cone.[168] So if the latter[169] is so small compared with the former, [D46] if the water, together with all the earth, is so little, measured against the size of the sun, how long would this small amount last in providing sustenance for so much fire? But in fact we see that the sea's flood-tide always comes up to the same level, and that river courses always remain within their own limits. The evidence that nothing of what is wet is consumed comes from this sort of observation. At the outset fire did not have its origin in the consumption of water; it, too, had its origin in the same power.[170] Correspondingly, the continuing existence of the element is based on its initial constitution; the wet nature is in no way adversely affected by that continuing existence of fire.

33. But, he[171] says, we see that the earth is often made

166. "Other" is not in the Greek.

167. Of the earth.

168. This notion goes back to Aristarchus of Samos (3rd century BCE), who used the concept of the sun's light as a cone to explain how the sun illuminated the moon and to calculate the relative sizes of the earth and the sun. See Risch, 203–4, n. 263.

169. The earth.

170. This rather obscure expression presumably refers to the discussion in §31; as explained there, fire has its own innate and peculiar power to stay in existence, without requiring the destruction of another nature such as water.

171. Basil; Gregory is paraphrasing *hom* 3.7.

wet by a downpour, but that what shortly before had been sodden becomes dry, as the more powerful heat of the sun warms what lies below it. Where then, he asks, is the wetness[172] that was there, unless it has been completely used up by the heat of the sun's beams? But if water in one pot is transferred to another and the one that was full suddenly becomes empty because the water is no longer in it, do people really say that the water that is now in the second pot has totally ceased to exist? Anyone who assumes that what was in the second pot is that which was in the first will not be far short of what is probably true! In the same way what is wet[173] flows across from one hollow place to another, and the earth's moisture[174] [D47] is dried out and lifted up into the air; it is natural that what is wet should seep upward from the earth in fine particles[175] when the warmth that lies above it draws it towards itself.

34. A proof of this process is provided by the fact that as the vapors given up from the depths of the earth become thicker, a cloudy structure seems to spring into existence, and the thickness of the vapors becomes such that it is accessible to our eyes. Sometimes there is some exhalation of moisture in smaller particles, of a size more or less equal to those of air; they do not appear to our sight until the exhalation of wet particles combines together and thus, through compression, they become a cloud. Because of their lightness, the fine and vaporous

172. "Wetness" (ὑγρότης) is here again a synonym of water.

173. τοῦ ὑγροῦ, another synonym for water.

174. τὴν νοτίδα, another synonym for water.

175. λεπτομερῶς. In later sections, Gregory frequently uses the cognate word μόριον, which I usually translate similarly as "particle." See introduction, n. 62, for possible "atomism" here.

particles of moisture[176] float in the air and are carried along by the winds; but if the common quality of the wet element[177] makes it flow more closely together and become heavy, it falls out of the air onto the earth and becomes raindrops.

35. So heat did not consume what it took up from the earth, but it was from that material[178] that the cloud was formed. When the cloud was compressed together, it became water.[179] That was then again mixed with earth, and dissipated[180] as vapor [D48], and the vapor, turned into a cloud, became rain. Then the earth again brought forth the vapors, and they, having thickened up to form the [M96] structure of the clouds, flowed down. Then what had been precipitated was given up again in vapors. So there is a kind of cycle, reversing back on itself, with a constant and repeated rotation and turning around.[181] Think of[182] plants and their shoots; they all go round in the same cycle. In plants and seeds the moisture rose up together with the shoots. Then it abandons to the mass of the growing plant whatever earthly material has accompanied it, and, when the substance of the plant is dried out by what surrounds it,[183] the moisture is exhaled back

176. "Particles of moisture" = τὰς ἰκμάδας (yet another synonym for water).

177. τοῦ ὑγροῦ again; see n. 173 above.

178. Literally, "from them."

179. That is, rain.

180. Following Drobner's reading ἀνεχέθη; PG and Forbes have the easier reading ἀνήχθη ("drawn up"). As Drobner (*ad loc.*) points out, ἀνεχέθη occurs in a similar context in §53 (see n. 236).

181. Literally, "and always rotating (περιχωρῶν) and turning around (ἑλισσόμενος) through the same things."

182. Literally, "If you speak of ..."

183. That is, the air, as the next sentence makes clear.

into its natural condition. Air is loosely textured in its individual particles, which are finer than the particles of the vapor,[184] and releases everything that is in it back to what is kindred to it. So dust too, even if widely dispersed through the air, is given back to the earth. Moisture is not destroyed but, wandering through the air, finds something of a similar kind, related to it; it attaches itself to that, grows bigger as the like things come together,[185] and swells to form the structure of a cloud. So, through raindrops, it is restored to its own natural condition; everywhere the components of the world which can be distinguished as separate elements within the whole are maintained in the same quantities [D49] as those that the wisdom of the Creator ordained at the outset for everything that is, so that everything might properly cohere together.

36. But I know what objections can be brought against this. For in the warmth of summer it is often possible to see clouds being dispersed through the atmosphere; if one scrutinized them further, the idea that nothing of the wet nature is used up would appear to be refuted. For the lumpy bits of the cloud are often scattered through the air in many places, and then, baked by the overpowering heat of the sun, first become smaller in size and then, dried up by the heat, completely disappear, as the heat of the sun desiccates the moisture and not even the smallest remnant is left. But that can no longer be left to be explained by reference to the rational principle that

184. Although in §34 Gregory has said that the particles of air and vapor are of more or less the same size.

185. For the principle of like being attracted to like, see introduction, n. 61.

underlies vapor.[186] For the state of things above the cloud, lying on top of this turbulent and windy air, will, in the subtlety of its own characteristic nature, receive nothing that is heavier than it. All vapors and all exhalations have as the limit of their upward movement the thickness of that part of the air that surrounds the earth; nature does not permit them to pass through that to what is above. For nothing composed of thick particles would survive in that subtle and airy region. Thus those who have investigated these matters[187] say that the high ridges of some very large mountains are always above the clouds, that they cannot be reached by winds, and that it is impossible for birds to fly there, just [D50] as underwater creatures cannot live in the air. So it is clearly demonstrated by all this evidence[188] that in the air there is some boundary between it and the place that lies above it,[189] which provides a spatial limit to all those things composed of thick particles that are exhaled from the earth. It is for this reason that snow on the high mountain ridges remains unmelted until the summer season; the accumulation of vapors in those parts constantly cools the air.

37. Those natural philosophers who are wise in these matters say that those fiery tracks which some call shoot-

186. Τοῦτο δὲ οὐκέτι ἐστὶ τῷ τῶν ἀτμῶν λόγῳ παραμυθήσασθαι. Gregory seems to mean that in this case the heated vapor cannot just do what one would on the face of it assume, that is, resolve itself into smaller and smaller particles and keep moving upward, because, as he goes on to explain, those particles could never become small enough to penetrate the upper atmosphere.

187. οἱ ἱστορήσαντες. Risch (206, n. 277), following Gronau, suggests that Gregory may have Posidonius in mind.

188. Literally, "through all things," διὰ πάντων.

189. That is, the highest "ethereal" part of the atmosphere: see next section.

ing stars arise from the same cause. When through the force of certain winds some of the thicker and more substantial air overflows into the ethereal region, as soon as it reaches this higher place it bursts into flame.[190] Through the impetus given to it by the wind, the flame [M97] is made to flow along; once the wind stops blowing, the flame dies down as the wind does.[191]

38. If then it is no longer possible to say that when the cloud disappears the vapors come together again, and for us to expect that, as is observed here in the lower world, the wet element that has been carried up returns and is restored to its original state,[192] we must agree with those who teach the doctrine that the wet element is burnt up [D51] and reduced to nothing.[193] I am persuaded that the wetness[194] in the vapors disappears through the fiery heat that overwhelms it, as I think it would be pointlessly contentious to seek to contest what is obvious. But since, even if that is so, it is nonetheless appropriate that those who are tracking down the truth should not become weary, I say that the measure of the wet nature[195] is preserved undiminished, and that what is consumed is always totally replaced in what remains.

190. Because the ether is fiery in nature.

191. This section is by way of a short excursus to illustrate how another natural phenomenon is affected by the division of the atmosphere into relatively heavy and ethereal regions.

192. "To its original state" is not in the Greek.

193. But, Gregory is arguing, it *is* possible so to say and so to expect (as explained in subsequent sections), so we must *not* agree with those, like Basil, who believe that "the wet element" (water) is "consumed" by fire. See part 6.3 of the introduction, pp. 36–39.

194. "Wetness" here means the quality, rather than being a synonym for water. Compare next note.

195. That is, the measure, or quantity, of water that was established in the original creation; see the antepenultimate sentence in §31 above.

39. What, for me, makes such a theory a secure one is this. In the activity of fire here among us, we discover by experience that fire does not devour all the qualities of the material it seizes on. Take as an example the material of oil: when in this material the wet is separated from the quality of cold, it is easily drawn up by the heat of fire and becomes a flame. But not only is the oil changed by the fire into flame, but it also becomes, after the flame, dry ash.[196] The way the smoke from a lamp blackens what lies above the flame clearly demonstrates this; if this process continues for a longer time, a sort of solid mass grows up in the place that has been blackened by the smoke. It is clear from this that the oil, when it has been dried out by the fire, is changed into fine and invisible particles; in this form it is in the air, from whence it settles onto the earth. What also demonstrates that there is a diffusion of fine particles of smoke in the air is the fact that the nostrils [D52] of those who breathe in this air become rather black, and what is spat up from the inside of the chest is often observed to be black by virtue of the color of the smoke, it too having had its color changed by what has slipped down into it through the breathing in of air. So it is clear from all this, that what is wet in the oil is changed into dryness, and that its material mass is scattered through the air in subtle and invisible particles, rather than vanishing into non-existence.

196. I follow previous versions in not translating the words τὸ τοῦ πυρὸς τοῦ γενομένου ἀπὸ τοῦ ἐλαίου φησίν ὑγρόν, found in various versions in the mss. and incorporated (with a warning footnote) in Drobner's text. With their inclusion, the second clause of the sentence would mean, "... but also, he says, the wet element of the fire that comes from the oil becomes, after the flame, dry ash." The words may be part of a scribal gloss accidentally incorporated into the text.

40. So what we have learned about this wetness from the action of things in the created world is that it is only the wetness that is changed into dryness; what is material does not completely disappear. If you came to the same conclusion about the totality of things, you would not be wrong, because it is clear that the whole emerges from its parts.[197] What we learned when considering a part also provides us with a lesson about the whole. For none even of the captious would deny that wetness is generically one. Yet wetness, burnt by fire, becomes fine ash; indeed, everything that is wet, when it is introduced to fire, is transformed from wet to dry and changes the quality of its particles, rather than vanishing altogether.

41. So since the cloud is a structure made from vapor, and vapor is the exhalation of fine particles of what is wet, it is absolutely necessary that, when [D53] the cloud is burnt up by the fiery heat, each subtle and indivisible particle[198] of the vapor, even though it does not keep its wet nature, is not dissolved into nothing and does not change, as regards its substance, into nothing. Four properties can be observed [M100] in vapor: wetness, coldness, weight, and quantity.[199] Of these, those that are in opposition to fire disappear by virtue of the power of the quality that overpowers them: neither wetness nor coldness remains as it is when it is in the fire. But quantity is a

197. That is, what is true of one wet thing is true of all of them.

198. ὄγκον. Normally "mass," but used to mean "particle" by the Epicureans (see Liddell & Scott, s.v. ὄγκος, B.III). For another use of ὄγκος in this sense, see §49, n. 229. Gregory normally uses μόριον for "particle"; see n. 175 above.

199. According to Aristotle, the four primary qualities are hot, cold, wet, and dry; Gregory adds quantity and weight. See part 6.3 of the introduction, pp. 36–37.

property that is naturally attributable to the substance of fire too. For "how much?" is a question that presents itself in the case of fire too, and there can be no inconsistency between the question "how much?" and the concept of quantity.[200] So if the quantity of the vapor is preserved when it has been separated from the qualities of wetness and coldness, and the quality of weight, which is naturally inherent to the substance of vapor, is preserved together with that of quantity—for weight is found equally in wet things and dry things—then our mind would not need too much effort to follow the sequence of things and recognize how, when water becomes earth through the transformation of the qualities of the vapor, it assumes an identical nature. For dryness and weight are characteristic of the quality that we see in the earth—that is what the vapor is changed into when it is burned out.[201]

42. It seems right to me that those who have adopted this starting point should not reject what follows sequentially from their inquiry; that is, what [D54] science,[202] which guides us towards truth, is moving towards, by considering what is probable. It is likely that it is for this reason that the sea constantly remains within its own boundaries: there is always a gradual addition of water to it, but then there is a draining out into the area above it through vapor, as the heat that warms the surface draws up the fine particles of the wet nature as a medical cupping device does. The coldness of the environment in inland or northerly parts may seem inconsistent with this

200. Literally, "For fire too is observed in the 'how much?' and quantity does not fight with the 'how much.'"

201. By the sun.

202. ἡ θεωρία.

notion, since the fact that the sea is not much warmed in those regions would be expected to prevent the upward release of the vapors. It is possible to lessen the force of this objection by two arguments. First, the sea is something single and completely continuous, nowhere cut off from contact with itself even when it is divided into a thousand bodies of water. So if the southern sea becomes excessively warm through the continuing presence of heat, the reduced quantity of water there will be perceptible in the parts that have been cooled down; because of its natural downward tendency, the flow of the water will be towards the area which is being constantly emptied.[203] Then too [D55] there is similar evidence that it is because of the upward release of vapors from the whole body of water that the sea is universally salty. For dryness is a characteristic of the nature of salt. If this quality is mixed equally with the whole of the sea, then saltiness will manifest its characteristic effects equally in every part. For every nature invariably produces effects appropriate to its own potentiality. For as fire burns and snow makes things cold and honey makes things sweet, so salt makes things dry. The drying nature of salt is everywhere mixed with the seas, God's wisdom having made this provision to facilitate the upward release of the vapors; for the saltiness of the water somehow squeezes and forces out the fine particles from the sea, prevailing over the

203. Drobner, following most mss., reads κινούμενον (normally "being moved"), as do PG and Forbes. Risch (211, n. 297) prefers κενούμενον, which Forbes says is found as a correction in one ms. All, however, translate as if the Greek read κενούμενον, "being emptied." I follow Risch, but perhaps κινούμενον is right, used in the sense of "removed": see Lampe, s.v. κινέω, I.A.2 and II.A.

wetness through the nature of dryness that it has within it. So one can think it probable that the consumption of the wetness occurs equally everywhere, as the air [M101] draws up the sea through vapors. That all the moisture in the air turns into cloud, and that from there storms of rain pour upon the earth, is shown by the earlier argument.[204] The teaching of the prophecy attributes this sort of activity to God, when it says, "he who calls for the water of the sea and pours it out on the face of the earth,"[205] and many other similar things. And we have learned from observing [D56] what actually happens: that all clouds are baked and completely dried up by the heat that lies above it.[206]

43. But we still must not pass over the objection that arises as a consequence of what we have already said.[207] Anyone who has followed the previous investigations will say that we have learned from the example of oil that in that case,[208] even after having been subject to considerable heat, what is material in a substance is not destroyed,

204. §34.

205. Am 5.8, 9.6.

206. See §§36 and 38.

207. That is, Basil's view that there is an excess of water in the universe to compensate for that which is destroyed by fire; see §28 above. "What we have already said" cannot refer specifically to the arguments that Gregory has already deployed against that theory, but rather to his general discussion of the phenomenon of evaporation and precipitation and how it should be interpreted. The whole of this section is Gregory's account of the view of Basil and his followers.

208. "In that case" is not in the text, but it may be the best way of representing the antithesis between the cases of oil and water that Gregory seems to be expressing by the use of μὲν and δὲ in this sentence and the subsequent one: literally, "the material element of a substance, on the one hand, is not destroyed.... But when wetness, on the other hand, disappears into the opposite quality ..."

but, through the action of fire, it is turned into earth and passes into the air. But when wetness disappears into the opposite quality, how is it possible for the wet nature to remain forever undiminished, when the hot substance burns away the wetness in the vapors and changes it to the quality of dryness, as the theory which follows sequentially from our previous investigations demonstrates? If therefore the wetness is drawn up as vapor, and, divided into subtle and indivisible parts through vaporization, becomes subject to the influence of the heat,[209] it is absolutely necessary to believe that the truer explanation,[210] when the wetness moves across into the quality of dryness, is that there is a surplus of water that constantly replenishes what has been consumed by fire. Perhaps one could get some support from Scripture for such a theory: the opening of the cataracts of heaven when the whole earth had to be flooded, with the water so deep that it overtopped every mountain peak.[211]

[D57] 44. But I say that it is possible to challenge the objection from Scripture by means of[212] another Scriptural text. I know that the divine words can sometimes refer to something other than what they normally refer to in Scripture. What does Scripture mean by "open," and what is signified by "shut"? It is clear that what has been shut can be opened and what has been opened can be shut. So when in the time of Elijah drought prevailed,

209. "Subject to the influence of" translates εὐάλωτος, literally, "easy to be caught by" or "easily affected by."

210. For those who accept Basil's theory.

211. See Gn 7.11 and 7.19–20.

212. εἶναιδιά on p.57, line 1, of Drobner's text is clearly a misprint for εἶναι διά.

Scripture says, "The heaven was shut up for three years and six months,"[213] I think that the words of the text are saying that the cataracts of heaven—that same heaven that was shut up[214] during the lack of rain—had been opened. But then, through Elijah's prayers, a cloud arose from the sea, and opened heaven for them in the heavy downpour of rain.[215] It can be clearly seen from this that not even then was the firmament of heaven pierced, with the rain streaming down from the waters that are said to be above it. Rather, by "heaven" is meant the air that surrounds the earth and provides a border for the place where vapors are found, that is, the border of the region above the earth where the finest particles can naturally be found.[216] Nothing of heavier nature can rise above that border, neither cloud, nor wind, nor vapor, nor exhalation, nor [D58] the nature of birds. Scripture normally means by "heaven" that which lies above our head; it calls those creatures who fly through the air "birds of heaven."[217]

45. But even if this is so, our argument has not yet resolved the other question, [M104] how, by the transformation of the vapors into a dry condition, the wet element is not diminished, consumed by the dominance

213. Lk 4.25; see also 1 Kgs 17.1, 18.1.

214. I follow Drobner here, who reads ὃς ἐκλείσθη; thus ὃς must refer to ὁ οὐρανός. PG and Forbes have ὡς ἐκλείσθη, "since the heaven was closed ..." The argument is not altogether clear on either reading, but Gregory seems to be illustrating the principle set out in the previous sentence, that to say that something is closed necessarily implies that it has been, or can be, opened.

215. 1 Kgs 18.44–45.

216. Literally, "the border of the nature that has the finest particles of what lies above."

217. Gn 1.26.

of the hot substance. For this purpose it would be good to discover another argument from sequence,[218] one that is consonant with the interpretation of the text. Perhaps by laborious attention we might succeed in finding an appropriate hypothesis to address the problem. Have you heard the prophecy that expounds the greatness of God's power by reference to the wonders of his creation, when it says, "Who has measured the water in his hand, and the heaven with a span, and all the earth in a grasp? Who has weighed the mountains in scales,[219] and the woodland vales in a balance?"[220] I think that the prophet clearly teaches that each of the elements is circumscribed within its own measure; the all-embracing power of God, which he calls God's "hand" and "span" and "grasp," closely binds each individual existing thing within the appropriate measure. If the heaven has been measured by the power of God, and water by his hand, and all the earth by his grasp, and the woodland vales weighed in the balance [D59], and a clear weight[221] defined for the mountains, it is absolutely necessary that everything should remain within its own measure and weight; there can be neither augmentation or diminution in those things that have been measured by God and circumscribed by him.

46. So if the prophecy provides evidence that there is neither increase nor reduction in respect of things that exist, everything remains forever in the measure appro-

218. Literally, "another sequence."

219. τίς ἔστησε τὰ ὄρη σταθμῷ; see n. 221.

220. Is 40.12.

221. ... καὶ φανερὸς τοῖς ὄρεσιν ἀφορίζεται σταθμός. See n. 219: the sense here requires σταθμός to be translated "weight," rather than as "scales" as in the quotation from Isaiah.

priate to it, although the changeable nature which we observe in those things is subject to reciprocal alteration, with each thing being changed into the other and then returning again, by change and alteration, from that condition to the original one. But when this wet vapor is exposed to fiery heat, becomes dry by being thoroughly baked, and is changed into an earthy quality, this can be adequately understood by the example of oil discussed earlier. But it is appropriate to investigate what happens next, whether, when the material of the vapor has changed into the opposite quality, it is possible for the remains of the vapor [D60] to remain above, as something that reason can apprehend, changed as it is by being thoroughly baked into something more subtle and less visible.

47. But I think it is possible to make conjectures about that too, using the examples known to us. For in the case of oil[222] the subtle particles of smoke do not remain forever in the air, but, because of the low density of the air, they are dispersed towards something of a similar nature and become attached to the floor, the walls, or the rafters of the roof. So it follows from the principle of sequence that one can assume the same in the current case, that the vapor too, driven up by the winds to the fiery place that lies above it, preserves its material component in the change that its wet nature undergoes; it becomes dry, and is then drawn down to what is of a similar nature and returned to the earth. Every existing thing has naturally within it a power that attracts it to things of the same nature, so it is not incompatible with the principle

222. Literally, "For there," ἐνταῦθα.

of sequence to assume that when vapor becomes dry and earthy, the quality of earth is mixed in with it. If everything wet had an oily nature, thoroughly baking vapors of this sort would, because of the coarse quality of their particles, change their color to black; it would be clearly apparent [M105] to everyone what had happened [D61], because they had assumed this form. But when it is the most subtle and transparent quality of the nature of water that comes to the fore in the vapors,[223] and the latter, having got rid of their wet quality in the fire, are changed into something dry, in line with the principle discussed earlier, it is absolutely necessary to think of them as having the characteristics of purity and airiness; it is only our intellect that can conceive that characteristic, for, because of its subtle quality, it eludes our observation.

48. But if anyone thinks that perception is more reliable than conceiving of something through reason, and seeks to see with their eyes those indivisible and invisible masses, they can, if they wish, see the air full of such particles when a sunbeam pours[224] through a window and makes visible whatever in the air is illuminated by its beam. For what in the rest of the air is inaccessible to our eyes is seen in the sunbeam, moving around in an innumerable quantity in the air. If anyone applies one's eyes to these, they will find that the direction of flow of those subtle particles is always downward. What appears in this portion of the air is a proof that the same thing happens universally, since everything is continuous with itself and

223. Literally, "comes to be (γίνεται) in the vapors."

224. εἰσχεθεῖσα διὰ θυρίδος ἀκτὶς. εἰσχεθεῖσα is presumably from εἰσχέω, although I cannot find evidence for this form of the passive aorist participle of χέω.

the whole is completed by its parts. If everywhere the direction of flow through the air of these subtle and indivisible particles is downward to the earth—it is clear that it is not the physical form of the ether that is broken up into these particles and dispersed, since the [D62] nature of fire[225] does not admit being broken up in this way into subtle particles and then being spread around—then it is absolutely necessary to believe that their material component descends, in the same way as, according to the theory that we have argued, they ascended in vapors.[226] So when they are wet, they are drawn up by the warm nature; then, after having been baked in the heat and become earthy, they are no longer held captive by the fire but are returned again to the earth.

49. Here is an analogy.[227] What we eat is changed inside us by digestion into a sort of subtle quality. It moves to a particular[228] part of the body by the process of distribution, and what has been distributed provides an increase to that part. In the constitution of the body there is a variety of differences between the parts, in dryness and wetness and heat and cold. Each part of what we eat turns into what naturally underlies that part of the body; at the appropriate time the dominant quality con-

225. The ether is fiery in nature; see §37.

226. Literally, "whose ascent the argument theorized through the vapors": ὧν τὴν ἄνοδον ὁ λόγος διὰ τῶν ἀτμῶν ἐθεώρησεν.

227. These words are not in the Greek, which consists of a single sentence beginning, "As what we eat," followed by a long series of subordinate clauses and genitive absolutes, and then, as the main clause, "in the same way, the perpetual increase in the earth through these indivisible masses is imperceptible." This would be very difficult to follow literally rendered into English, so I have split it into separate sentences, adding this explanatory introduction.

228. "Particular" is not in the Greek.

verts the subtle nature of what has been distributed to it into itself. In the same way, the perpetual increase in the earth through these indivisible particles[229] is imperceptible.[230] So whatever coalesces with whatever lies below it changes its nature into what that which receives it is, in its substantial being: if it is in a clod of earth, it becomes a clod of earth; if in sand, sand; if in stone, stone, and so in all similar cases; whenever what receives it is something solid, it is changed into whatever is the dominant quality.

[D63] 50. If, however, anyone thinks that the hardness of stone would not permit this sort of increase, even though that would follow by logical sequence, I myself do not think it is necessary to raise any objection to those who take that view. My theory does not become any less probable; the flow of earthy material from above is transferred by the winds from what will not receive it to what it can coalesce with.[231]

51. But someone may perhaps say that our argument does not support what it purports to prove:[232] that it sets out to show that the wet nature remains forever in its original quantity, but it inadvertently proves the opposite. [M108] It may be that what has been sent upward remains within the fire; it may be that it is dried up and returns again to the earth. In either case there will be a reduction in the quantity of water; this phenomenon in no way disproves the necessity that there should be a to-

229. ὄγκων: see n. 198 above.

230. Literally, "the perpetual increase in the earth is imperceptible through (because of) these indivisible particles."

231. That is, from impermeable stone to porous soil.

232. Literally, "does not look towards its own objective."

tal excess of the wet element, because it is forever being consumed away.

52. So in response to this argument it will be necessary again to consider the nature of created things, so that, by understanding that nature[233] our investigation may be properly directed towards its proposed objective.

53. What then is that nature? None of what we observe as constituent elements of the universe that surrounds the earth were made immovable and unchangeable by the Creator of all. Rather, everything is in everything else, while distinct from everything else; the transforming power [D64], through a sort of cyclical motion, changes all earthly things into each other and then changes them back from each other into themselves. This process of change operates constantly in the elements, so that it is absolutely necessary that things are transformed into each other and then in the same way change back again and return to what they were. None of these elements would be able to maintain its identity[234] unless mixture with something of another kind sustained its nature.[235] How, someone might ask, does the changing and transforming power in the four elements give effect to its circular course? For not everything comes into being through other things, nor does the cycle of transfor-

233. Literally, "through it (the nature)." The discussion that follows in §§53–57 is based on the same Aristotelian principles as is that in §§38–41; see part 6.3 of the introduction, pp. 36–38.

234. Literally, "be preserved in itself," φυλαχθείη.

235. The thought here is that the continuing existence of the universe depends on change, a philosophical commonplace that goes back to Heraclitus. There must be a continuous transformation of one element into another, as in the Aristotelian system which Gregory adapts; otherwise, the elements would indeed eliminate each other by their mutual antagonism. See Risch, 214, n. 323.

mation revolve equally through all beings; water is dissipated[236] into the air through vapors; the vapors feed the fire[237] and then turn into earth, becoming a sort of ash after having come into contact with the fire; the earth receives it and then itself brings the process of transformation to an end. The question of whether the nature of water takes its origin from the earth has not yet been investigated.

54. So this remains to be considered, whether it is possible for earth to change its nature into that of water. No one would accuse us of hair-splitting if we investigated how it was possible for the principle of sequence [D65] to apply to what we have said. Now we observe many dry things that, because of some natural characteristic, become wet. One can see this in the case of salt, whether it has been mined or has emerged from the drying out of something wet. Its characteristic condition is to be dry, but when some salt comes into contact with what is humid, it becomes moist and changes its inherent dryness into the quality of wetness. In the same way I have noted that the nature of honey somehow becomes dry when it is baked, but that it then, in response to a particular environment, melts and becomes wet again.

55. But let that pass. It is better to establish that our

236. ἀνεχέθη: see n. 180 above.

237. As Risch (215, n. 325) points out, this seems inconsistent with what Gregory says in §§28–32, that the fire does not consume the water. As I understand Risch's not altogether clear suggestion, it is that Gregory uses the concept of feeding here not to imply that one thing is consumed by another but rather to emphasize that things cannot remain in stable opposition or contradiction with each other; they must rather move or change in response to each other, and that movement and change can be compared with the process of feeding.

theory follows the principle of sequence by deriving it from some necessary first principle. We do not perceive a common quality in each of the elements, through which its substance is brought to its complete realization[238] and distinguished from its fellows. Each thing is comprehended through different qualities: in some cases those qualities have nothing in common with each other; in others, they are observed as being equal, with a fitting harmony between the mutually competing qualities. For example, in the case of earth and water, dryness and wetness are not mixed with each other, but coldness is associated with both of them and somehow in [M109] itself brings the conflicting qualities into one. Again, water is separated from air by the opposition of heaviness and lightness, but here too coldness can be observed equally in the nature of both, and mediates between them.[239] Yet again, air is distinguished from fire by the opposition of heat and cold, but they have the quality of [D66] lightness in common,[240] and that common quality is, as it were, a reconciler between the opposition of their natures. And then fire is separated from earth by virtue of the qualities of weight and lightness, but dryness is common to both, and so the separate qualities are brought into a sort of alliance.

56. What should be my aim in starting further investigations? For coldness can be observed in earth, water,

238. Literally, "is fulfilled," συμπληροῦται.

239. Gregory departs from Aristotle in making air cold rather than hot; see also §56.

240. In order for Gregory's theory of transformation between the elements to work in the case of fire (hot, dry) and air (cold, wet), he has to posit the common quality of lightness (κουφότης); see part 6.3 of the introduction, pp. 36–38.

and air, although for the most part it is characteristic of water. It somehow preserves the nature of water within itself, and through its antipathy to heat limits the contrary effect of dryness. As dryness clings closely to the heat, and fire cannot be shown to be in only one of these,[241] so it is fair to say that coldness is united with wetness, because in each of the things that can be observed in both fire and water, the opposite characteristic must be present, so that wetness is opposed to dryness, and cold to heat.[242] If it were to be shown that coldness, just as much as wetness, formed an essential part of the nature of water, it would follow in logical sequence that, as the quality of coldness is also naturally present in earth, water is potentially in earth, and earth is potentially in water. The bond that the wetness has with the coldness in the nature of each of these elements does not allow one to be unyoked from the other. Rather, even when one of these elements is found alone and by itself, it is not strictly speaking alone; potentially both elements can be seen in the one.[243] When [D67] wetness is diffused into the air, the particles of vapor become cold as a result; so, in the opposite way, when coldness dwells in the depth of the earth, the wetness is not absent from the quality with which it is linked; it is natural that the cold potentiality lies within the earth and becomes like a seed of the wet nature. Through itself it constantly generates the quality that is joined to it; the

241. Heat or dryness.

242. Dryness helps stop fire from becoming cold in the same way that coldness helps stop water from becoming dry.

243. In the preceding two sentences the word "element" (i.e., earth or water) and the words "of each of these" (elements) are not in the Greek.

transformative activity, through excessive cooling, changes the earth to make it produce water.

57. If anyone were to ask us for a rational account of how this transformation brings about a change from solidity to wetness, we would be as much at a loss as in any other similar case.[244] For how can water be dispersed into the air, how can what naturally tends downward float on what is light? How does the transformation change what is heavy into something light? When these things happen, we grasp them by perception, but are unable to represent these operations of nature to our reason.

58. If people were prepared to accept a practical example as evidence for this hypothesis, we could readily produce such evidence by drawing their attention to those who dig wells. In the case of the waters that are come across in the depths of the earth, when the well diggers dig through the dry earth and continue working downward, they do not immediately come across the body of water; rather, as they make successive contact,[245] they first discover that the earth is affected by a certain wetness. When, as they go further down, they reach a cooler place [D68], they come across more muddy soil. After that, when their work takes them down to an even[246] cooler place, traces of a sort of exudation[247] appear. Then a channel is cut below the base of the rock, and it can be expected that [M112] the heat of the sun can no longer penetrate there because it is blocked off by the thickness

244. Literally, "as for (ἐπὶ) all the others." A "similar case" is identified in the following sentence.

245. "As they make successive contact" translates τῇ ἁφῇ, literally, "by the touch."

246. "Even" is not in the Greek.

247. Literally, "a certain obscure exudation" (or "sweat").

of the rock. Then narrow veins of water are opened up by the work; these join together in a circle round the lowest point and there is plenty of water in the well. What happens there in an artificial cavity—all round the well the moisture is put under pressure and collects into one—may be expected to happen everywhere; small quantities of moisture keep coming together and are carried through veins into wider channels and as the small quantities flow into each other they become one. So this is how the water is produced: on the one hand, coldness makes the earth wet, and, on the other, wetness is produced from the cold, thus in itself bringing the full nature of water to completion. Now they are collected together and become a stream; if they can find a way out, they make an aperture in the earth there. This is called a spring.

59. A proof of the fact that coldness is what brings about the coming into being of water is that northerly regions, which are [D69] colder, abound in water; for certainly the sunny regions in the south would be soaked with water if the absence of cold presented no obstacle to the formation of water. When rainwater, collected together as individual drops flow into each other, becomes a torrent, if one were to look at the drops in themselves, each one would appear insignificant, nothing at all. In the same way, wetness emerges from minute quantities underground; when, passing through many different channels, the minute quantities are collected together into one, they emerge to form the nature of a river.[248]

248. Drobner has τὸ τοιοῦτον εἰς τοιοῦτον εἰς πηγὴν ἐκρήγνυται ("breaks out into a spring"), ἡ δὲ ποταμοῦ φύσιν ἐκδίδοται. Forbes and PG omit εἰς πηγὴν ἐκρήγνυται, which has little ms. support and looks like a scribal gloss. Drobner defends its inclusion on the basis of his dating

60. If people rejected these theories, what would they think was the origin of those rivers that flow uninterruptedly? Would they not suspect that there were pools of some sort in the deep recesses of the earth? But these too, unless they received an inflow, would become empty in a short time. So there must necessarily be thought to be some other pools feeding into them.[249] But the sequence of logical reasoning will seek out what in turn fills up [D70] those others; and if people assume that there are other pools which in turn feed into[250] them, they will necessarily investigate what causes these latter to be filled up. And so the argument will go on *ad infinitum*, never ceasing to posit pools beyond pools, lest pools to provide for the springs should ever run out. Eventually people will reach the sources of the final ones, where the creation of water has its origin.

61. It is reasonable to find out the cause of the original nature of water; for this purpose it would be much more sensible to reflect upon the formation of the springs, rather than to imagine underground lakes. Water's natural tendency to move downward can immediately be seen to be inconsistent with the latter explanation.[251] For how could something flow upward whose nature includes, as

of the relevant mss., but I nevertheless follow Forbes's text: τὸ τοιοῦτον (that is, the "collection," ἄθροισμα) εἰς ποταμοῦ φύσιν ἐκδίδοται.

249. ὥστε κατ' ἀνάγκην καὶ ἄλλας τούτων ὑπερκεῖσθαι νομίσαι. ὑπερκεῖσθαι means literally "to be situated above," which would present an odd picture of the relative positions of the two pools and is in any case inconsistent with what Gregory says in the next section. Risch, 219, n. 338, suggests that Gregory is using "above" here in the sense of "logically and causally prior," rather than in a topical sense. My translation aims to reflect that.

250. ὑπερκεῖσθαι: see previous note.

251. Literally, "immediately ... stands opposed to the explanation" (λόγον).

one of its characteristics, moving in a downward direction? Then again, whatever the size of those pools, would the continuous outflow of so much water give one to suppose that, after continuing at such a rate for such a long time, it would remain inexhaustible, if nobody replaced the water that came out?

62. It would become clear from research, however, that there is no shortage of water in the river. This is because the earth changes into water. But the mass of the earth is not made less [M113] by what comes out of it; the constant transformation of the dry vapors replenishes the perpetual diminution of the mass. When that happens, it seems [D71] to us that there is no longer any objection to the theory of the mutual transformation of the elements into each other.[252] Rather, the argument proceeds in a sequential way: it regards the change of each thing into the other as the origin of that into which it is transformed, and as its restoration back from that into what it was in the beginning. For example, water, dissipated[253] into the air through vapors, becomes air; the wet air is dried out in the flames that lie above it; through the nature of the fire, the earthy is separated from the wet; when it is once again in the earth, it is transformed into water by the quality of cold. And so the cyclical transformation of the elements into each other is continuous and unimpeded; none of them is either consumed or added to, but rather they each continually remain in the quantities measured out for them in the beginning.

252. Literally, "it seems to us that the transformation of the elements into each other no longer limps" (σκάζειν).

253. Drobner and Forbes have ἀναχθὲν ("drawn up"), but I follow Risch's reading (221, n. 342) of ἀναχεθέν. See nn. 180 and 236 above.

63. So, proceeding sequentially from our previous inquiries, we should consider that the waters situated above the firmament are not wet in nature, as we have established in what we have already said that the nature of fire is not sustained by the consumption of what is wet. It was shown in our previous inquiries that what is hot is not sustained by what is cold, but is extinguished by it, and what is dry is made to vanish, not increased, by what is wet.[254]

---

64. But it is now time to turn our consideration to the other matter we are inquiring into, how after the third day all the lights of the heaven were made.[255] A particular word of command from God brings about each of these wonderful events (Moses [D72] teaches us about these lofty doctrines through the medium of a historical account), as we have established in our earlier arguments. Through those arguments we came to know that the voice of God is not a command expressed through words, but that the word of God is that wise artisanal power found in everything that has come into existence, through which the wonders of existence[256] are given effect, and that it should be spoken of in that way. And we have come to know that everything was constituted simultaneously, in the plenitude[257] of creation, by God's initial will, and that the ordered series[258] that necessarily

254. This is the end of the fourth and longest part of *hex* (§§27–63), providing a detailed critique of Basil's idea that the waters above the firmament are material. The fifth part (§§64–76) interprets Gn 1.14–18.

255. See the discussion of this section in part 5.3 of the introduction, pp. 29–30.

256. Literally, "the wonders in things that are" (τοῖς οὖσι).

257. "Plenitude" is πλήρωμα: see also n. 261 below.

258. "Ordered series," here and at the end of this section, is τάξις.

arose, in consequence of the wisdom that is found within everything that exists, brought each of the elements into its manifestation as a consequence[259] of the divine commands. Moses was indicating the totality when he summarized it in an inclusive expression referring to the original coming into existence of the sensible creation: "In the beginning God created the heaven and the earth."[260] He says that God created the sum total[261] of things; he indicates in his account that the manifestation of each existing thing happened in a naturally ordered series.

65. Light came into being with everything else, but it was not immediately manifested before everything else, for as long as the non-luminous parts of creation obscured the illuminating power. But at the same time as creation was given God's signal to arrange itself in order,[262] the fiery and illuminating power of creation appeared first, in the [D73] subtlety and mobility of its[263] nature, leaping out before everything else. To begin with, it was all collected together in one and revolved around everything, but after that it divided itself back into individual particles, into what was appropriate to and of the same kind as itself. For it is clear from what can be observed that there is not just one potentiality in the nature of light, but that if, when people are referring to light in the generic sense, when it is all collected together, they call it "one," they are not wrong; in the creation narrative[264] the divine word uses the singular and refers to the

259. "Consequence" is ἀκολουθίαν.
260. Gn 1.1.
261. "Sum total" is πλήρωμα: see also n. 257 above.
262. "To arrange itself in order" is πρὸς τὴν διακόσμησιν αὐτῆς.
263. "Its" is not in the Greek, but must be understood here.
264. Literally, "in the beginning," καταρχὰς.

whole of light, commanding "light," not "lights," to come into being. If people look at actual phenomena, they will see a great difference in the potential power of light as manifested in the existing world. Thus the psalmist says: "To Him who alone made great lights,"[265] and the Apostle says, "There is one glory of the sun, [M116] and another glory of the moon, and another glory of the stars; indeed, star differs from star in glory,"[266] for there is indeed much difference within what is called "light."[267] Even if all the things that Paul enumerated give illumination, and each one is perceived in its own characteristic power and glory, it is proper to refer to all of them as one light, using the word generically, but to regard them as separate and unconfused with respect to the differences between them.[268]

66. If this is how things are, I do not think our assumption will be inconsistent with the principle of logical sequence if we assume that Moses thought that in the beginning all the illuminating power gathered together into one came into being as "light." Since [D74] in the subtle and mobile nature of all luminous things great differences, in addition to greater or smaller size, can be observed,[269] the separation of time supplied by the

265. Ps 135 (136).7.

266. 1 Cor 15.41.

267. Literally, "concerning light," κατὰ τὸ φῶς.

268. Literally, "to regard the difference that is in them as separate and unconfused."

269. Literally, "Since much difference in the subtle and the mobile, in addition to greater or smaller size (παρὰ τὸ μᾶλλον καὶ ἧττον), was observed in the nature of all (τῶν ὅλων)." The difference that Gregory is referring to is that between the "most completely subtle and light" part of the fire (see the next sentence), which forms the ether, and the "inactive and sluggish" parts that are broken up to form the heavenly bodies.

first three days was sufficient to bring about a clear and distinct mutual severance between each of these things. So the most completely subtle and light part of the fiery substance, the purely immaterial, is found in the highest part of sensible nature, the point where intellectual and incorporeal nature takes over, but all of the more inactive and sluggish part collects itself together, contained within the circuit of the subtle and light part. Then that is divided into seven,[270] according to the different individual characteristics that are innate within it; all the particles of light that correspond with each other and are of the same kind combine together because of their mutual similarity and are separated from what is of a different nature.[271]

67. So all these particles of the sun's nature are dispersed throughout the substance of light, but they come together with each other and become a single large thing. Similarly, in the case of the moon and all the other stars, both planets and those that are fixed; the coming together of the particles of each, like with like, creates one of the objects that appear,[272] and the same applies to all of them. The great Moses found it sufficient to mention by name only the best-known [D75] of these, the "greater

270. The reference is not to the seven known "planets" (Sun, Moon, Mercury, Venus, Mars, Jupiter, Saturn) but to the seven heavenly circles of fixed stars identified in Philo's *de opificio mundi* 112 (see Risch, 224, n. 356)—the Arctic and Antarctic circles, the summer and winter solstices (tropics of Cancer and Capricorn), the equator, the zodiac, and the Milky Way. He uses the same model in §§69 and 72; see nn. 278 and 284.

271. Gregory seems to be envisaging all the different kinds of particles potentially contained in the primordial unitary "light," being, as it were, sorted according to the particular heavenly body to which they are appropriate.

272. In the sky.

and lesser lights," and to refer to all the others generically as "stars."[273]

68. The grossness of our intellect may struggle, as it cannot keep up with the subtlety of the divine wisdom. But then[274] nobody[275] should be surprised when they consider the poverty of our nature; it must be content with not being infallible in any particular thing, but with at least being able to grasp the overall unity.[276]

69. I say that with reference to the question of what the rationale is for this space of three days, why that amount of time was sufficient for the dividing up into each of the luminous bodies that we see. It is absolutely clear that there must be some rationale, even if it is beyond the scope of our power of vision. It must be that this amount of time is appropriate to the dividing up of the nature of light. The separation of the "lights," their division into the individual lights of heaven, required the appropriate period of time and a certain quantity of dynamic force in the fire. So each of the innumerable differences between the "light" was distributed[277] to its proper position, to where, as provided by its particular nature, its inherent potentiality led it. There was no [M117] confusion or mixing up in all this, because it was by the divine wisdom that this separation took place. [D76] There was an inevitable ordering, based on the particular nature of each "light," so that those who had a greater ten-

273. Gn 1.16.

274. "Then" is not in the Greek.

275. I follow PG and Forbes, reading μηδεὶς. Drobner, without explanation, prefers the alternative ms. reading μηδὲν.

276. "Particular" and "overall" are not in the Greek.

277. Literally, "separated," ἀποκριθῆναι.

dency to rise upward than others with such a tendency reached the highest place; these were either allocated to the middle, or became southern or northern stars, or occupied the area in between, or populated the Milky Way or the zodiac;[278] then each brought to perfection its own individuality as a star. In the case of those stars found in a constellation, none is positioned randomly in its particular place,[279] but rather remains fixed and immutable in that part[280] to where its naturally inherent characteristics have led it, controlled by the power of its own nature, in accordance with the wisdom of him who made it.

70. When the mind observes things like that, it becomes dizzy and condemns its own stupidity; it cannot work out the rationale for how the period of three days can be sufficient for the dividing up of so many stars. Or how, given the infinite[281] distance between the fixed globe of the earth and the bodies that surround it, the great wisdom of God set [D77] the nature of the sun in the midst of all this expanse, so that we would not live completely in darkness; before the brightness that radiates from the stars comes to us, it is consumed in the intervening space, and it was for this reason that God's

278. See n. 270 for the model of seven heavenly circles of fixed stars which is assumed here. "The middle" is the equator, and the solstices (tropics) are "in between" the poles and the equator. Each circle seems to be associated with a separate concentric heavenly zone or sphere; see further in §72, n. 284.

279. Literally, "And again in the star (ἐν τῷ ἄστρῳ), each of the stars lying in a constellation [assuming that is what is meant by ἐν τῷ σχήματι κειμένων ἄστρων] does not have its position randomly either thus or thus." "In the star" seems a redundant phrase.

280. Of heaven.

281. ἄπειρον. As Risch (225, n. 361) points out, this cannot be taken literally; Gregory must mean "very great."

wisdom placed the power of the sun's brilliant nature at such a height above us that its rays would not be dimmed by a great distance but that neither would it cause us trouble by being too close. Or how the more thick and material of the heavenly bodies (I am talking about the lunar body) should be drawn down and revolve in the region next to the earth; it can be observed to have a sort of intermediate nature, participating equally in the non-luminous and the luminous power. The thickness of its substance blunts its native luminosity, but because of the reflection of the rays of the sun, it is not completely deprived of illuminating power.[282]

71. But the wretchedness of our nature is unable to see the rational principle of wisdom that can be seen in everything that exists. I believe, however, that it is possible for those who understand to a certain extent how to have regard to the principle of sequence, in some way to grasp, using some guesswork, how to perceive a certain sequence in the way things came into being, corresponding to the order which the Lawgiver imposed upon the creation of existing things.

[D78] 72. So let us take up again the sequence of how things came into being. This is how it was. Because of its mobile quality, generic and universal light appeared before everything else; then followed the outline of the firmament, bounded by the circular revolution of fire. The weightless nature having been separated from heavier things, the next in the sequence was the separation

282. Gregory follows the Stoic Cleomedes in holding that the moon, like the other heavenly bodies, has within it a natural luminosity of its own, even though this cannot be observed because of the opacity of its crust. See Risch, 225, n. 363.

from each other of the heavy qualities, divided into earth and water. When the nature of the things below had been put into order, the subtle and light substance high up in the sky, because it was not all of the same kind, was differentiated, in the separation brought about through the elapsing of time, from its common nature into things with individual, though similar, characteristics.[283] The innumerable multitude of the stars, unfolded in accordance with the individual nature of each particular one, hastened up to the highest point of creation, and each took up its own place. They do not cease from their ever-moving course, nor do they move from the place where they have been put; their arrangement has the quality of immovability, their nature that of perpetual movement. The nature that is the next [M120] fastest to that which moves most quickly adopts for its own course the circle immediately below the latter, and similarly with the third and fourth right down to the seventh; the distance each star is below the one above depends on its natural speed, on how tardy in movement its nature is, compared with those above it.[284]

[D79] 73. So this is what happened in the course of the fourth day; light was not created then, but the characteristics of light were assembled together in the naturally

283. Drobner and Forbes, as shown in their punctuation of the Greek and in Forbes's translation (p. 87), seem to take "in the separation brought about through the elapsing of time" with "because it was not all of the same kind." I follow PG and Risch (98) in taking it with "was differentiated," which seems to make more sense.

284. Each of the seven circles of fixed stars is associated with a series of concentric zones or spheres, containing in turn the zone of the seven planets. See Risch, 229, n. 372, with references to the astronomer Achilles's *Isagoga* 18 and Cicero's *de natura deorum* 2.52–53.

appropriate way.[285] The stars appeared and, among them, those that were perceived to be bigger in mass than the others, the sun and the moon; their coming into being had its origin in the initial constitution of light. Since everything that moves can be moved only in time and some period of time is required for the particles to coalesce with each other, it took three days for each heavenly body to be constituted. In the great Moses's account of the construction of things, nothing was written that went beyond the principle of sequence; for by the power of the Creator everything was established simultaneously in material form; then in order to bring actual things into existence, the individual manifestation of the objects we see in the universe was completed in a certain natural order and sequence, according to the prescribed interval of time. To begin with, it was light collectively that appeared, but now the whole nature of light shone through in its individual manifestations, among which are the sun and the moon.

74. Here is an analogy.[286] Everything that has the potential to flow flows, but not altogether in the same way. Rather, there are differences between different fluids, for example oil and water and [D80] quicksilver. If you pour them all together into a single vessel, when a short time has passed, you will first see the quicksilver, because it

285. Literally, "the characteristic of light (τῆς φωτιστικῆς ἰδιότητος, singular) was assembled around what was according to its own nature and appropriate [for the formation of each individual heavenly body]."

286. This sentence is not in the Greek, which comprises one single sentence from the beginning of this section to "... upward-tending nature" (in the translated text immediately preceding footnote number 287). Literally, "For just as everything that has the potential to flow flows ... thus I believe that we should form a similar view ..."

is heavier and more downward-tending than the other two, join together in all its individual particles, even if all these happen to have been scattered everywhere. Then the water concentrates itself together, and then the particles of oil float above everything that lies below them and cluster together. I believe that we should form a similar view in respect of the issue that lies before us, changing the analogy only as much as is necessary: we should look at what happens in fluids on account of weight, the opposite of what happens in the case of the upward-tending nature.[287] Simultaneously with the initial laying of the foundations for existing things, everything was carried upward because of its lightness, according to how much it had of the potential for speed that is inherent in everything. As a necessary consequence, each thing combined together with whatever was moving alongside it, and so was separated, by virtue of its difference in speed, from other things that had come into being, and been given their own potential, at the same time as they had. In the analogy the separation of the fluids that were mentioned did not, by drawing them apart, create specific material substances;[288] rather, it showed how each, having already come into existence, and mixed up with the others, was then cleanly separated, one from the other.[289] So, in the case of the heavenly bodies, the illuminating nature and

287. In fluids, heavier elements sink to the bottom because of their weight; in the created universe, light rises to the top because of its "upward-tending" nature.

288. "Specific material substances" = τὰς ὕλας.

289. "Already" and "then" are not in the Greek. Gregory is reinforcing the point that the heavenly bodies were not actually created on the fourth day, but were potentially there from "the initial laying of the foundations." This is made clearer in the next sentence.

power[290] of the sun did not come into existence after the three-day interval of time; rather, having been mixed up with everything else, it separated itself into itself.

[D81] 75. If you ask us for information about the third heaven, which Moses did not write about but which Paul saw and in which, finding himself as it were in secret sanctuaries of wisdom,[291] he heard things "not to be told,"[292] our reply is that that third heaven is not inconsistent with the conclusions [M121] to which our inquiries have led us.[293] It seems to me that the great Apostle, "straining" himself "forward" to everything that "lies ahead"[294] and having passed the frontier of all of sensible nature, penetrated into the intelligible realm; the vision that he had of intelligible things was not a corporeal one. He indicates this in his own words, when he says, "And I know that such a person—whether in the body or out of the body I do not know; God knows"—was "caught up" into the third heaven.[295] So I think Paul called the highest part of the sensible cosmos the "third heaven"; he divided the whole phenomenal world into three, and, following the normal usage of these texts, he called each of these divisions "heaven." The account in Scripture uses words in a somewhat unusual way when it calls the frontier of that part of the air that is composed of thicker

290. Literally, "So also, the illuminating nature and power …"

291. τῆς σοφίας, as read by PG, Forbes, and Risch (230, n. 377). Drobner reads τῇ σοφίᾳ.

292. 2 Cor 12.4.

293. Literally, "not outside what has been inquired into," ἔξω τῶν ἐξητασμένων.

294. ὁ πᾶσι τοῖς ἔμπροσθεν ἑαυτὸν ἐπεκτείνων. See Phil 3.13. This is the text that Gregory uses elsewhere to support his celebrated doctrine of "epectasis"—"straining forward" towards God.

295. 2 Cor 12.3–4, slightly altered.

particles, the limit to which clouds and winds and [D82] high-flying birds can naturally reach, the one "heaven." Scripture speaks of the clouds of heaven[296] and the birds of heaven[297] and in this context does not use only the word "heaven" but also "firmament." For it says, "Let the waters bring forth creeping things with living souls and birds flying above the earth across the firmament of heaven."[298] And then it speaks of another heaven and firmament, what can be observed within and immediately below the sphere of the fixed stars, where the planets have their courses. For it says, "And God made the ... great lights ... and placed them in the firmament of heaven, so as to shine upon the earth."[299] It is clear to anyone who has in any way considered the ordering of the whole universe how much their courses lie below that of those above them. And Scripture also calls the very summit of the sensible world, the boundary of the intelligible creation, "firmament" and "heaven."

76. So he who sought after what was above the scope of human reason,[300] and aiming, as we are enjoined to do, at things that are not seen (since "what can be seen is temporary, but what cannot be seen is eternal"),[301] came to where his desire raised him, lifted up by the power of him who had revealed to him what he should desire. And instead of saying, "I know a man [D83] who passed through the whole sensible creation and found himself

296. E.g., Dn 7.13, Mt 24.30.
297. Ps 103 (104).12.
298. Gn 1.20.
299. Gn 1.16–17.
300. Literally, "above λόγος."
301. 2 Cor 4.18.

in the secret sanctuaries of intelligible nature,"[302] since he had studied the Holy Scriptures from childhood, he used scriptural expressions to denote the intelligible world;[303] he calls passing through the three divisions that can be observed in the universe, the "third heaven." For he left the air behind; he passed through the intermediate orbits of the stars; he even went beyond the boundary where the ether reaches its limit. He found himself within the unmoving intelligible nature; he saw the beauties of paradise, and heard things that human nature does not utter.[304]

---

77. These are our answers, man of God, to those things that have been drawn to our attention by Your Sapience.[305] We have not turned any of the text of Scripture into allegory or metaphor, nor overlooked or left unexamined any of the objections which have been raised.[306] Rather, we have left the text's significance unchanged and, as far as possible, followed the logical order of nature by investigating the terms used. Thus [M124] we have, as far as possible, shown that things that seem on a superficial reading to be inconsistent are in fact not in

302. Cf. 2 Cor 12.2.

303. τὸ νόημα, picking up "intelligible (νοητῆς) nature" earlier in the same sentence.

304. Cf. 2 Cor 12.4. This ends the fifth and final substantive part of *hex.* The two final sections constitute a conclusion.

305. Τῆς συνέσεώς σου. Or possibly "your sapience" (or "wisdom"). See Risch, 232, n. 385, and cf. "Your Sagacity," τῇ φρονήσει σου, in §5 and "Your Sapience,"τῆς σῆς συνέσεως, in §78.

306. μήτε παριδόντες τι τῶν ἀντιτεθέντων ἡμῖν ἀνεξέταστον. This may refer to the objections raised against Basil mentioned in §§3 and 5 (thus Risch, 232–33, n. 387), or to those raised against Gregory himself, for example in §36, or perhaps to both.

conflict with each other. To go through the rest of the things [D84] created in the six days of cosmogony we have judged to be pointless, as the sublime voice of our teacher did not leave out of his consideration any of the issues that need investigation, with the exception of the fashioning of humankind; we sent Your Perfection a book dedicated to that topic,[307] which we had labored on before this one. In this book and in that one we ask you and every reader not to think that we are setting ourselves up in opposition to the laborious work of our teacher. Think, rather, that we are filling up the gaps in it by adding some speculations about humankind to his laborious work on the six days and that we are eager, for the sake of those who look for sequence in the thoughts expressed in Scripture, to demonstrate this in what we write,[308] so as both to preserve the actual wording of Scripture and to harmonize the theory of natural philosophy with the letter of the text.

78. If there are defects in what I have said, I have no problem with what is lacking being filled out either by Your Sapience or by any other reader. For the two obols donated by the widow did not mean that the wealthy cannot offer their gifts,[309] nor were those who brought Moses skins, wood, and hair for the construction of the tabernacle any hindrance to those who contributed gold and silver and precious stones.[310] We too will be content if what we offer [D85] is reckoned to be in the same class as hair,

307. On "the fashioning of humankind": see part 1 of the introduction, p. 5.

308. Literally, just "to write this."

309. See Mk 12.41–42.

310. See Ex 35.4–9.

provided only that, by making use of your purple woven together with gold, the overgarment is added to the treatise, the overgarment whose name is Oracle and Manifestation and Truth,[311] as Moses says when he furnishes the priest with such covering, acting on the instructions of God. To whom, together with the only-begotten Son and the Holy Spirit, glory and power are due, unto the ages of ages. Amen.

311. λόγιόν τε καὶ δήλωσις καὶ ἀλήθεια. See LXX Ex 28.26 (= 28.30 in modern English translations). The "overgarment" is the priestly breastplate (called λογεῖον, "oracle," in LXX Ex 28.15; λογίον is another form of λογεῖον). "Manifestation" and "Truth" are what in the Hebrew text are called "the Urim and the Thummim."

INDICES

GENERAL INDEX

INDEX OF HOLY SCRIPTURE

Old Testament

New Testament

WRITINGS OF ST. GREGORY OF NYSSA IN THE FATHERS OF THE CHURCH SERIES

Ascetical Works, translated by Virginia Woods Callahan, Fathers of the Church 58 (1967)

Life of Gregory the Wonderworker, in *St. Gregory Thaumaturgus: Life and Works,* translated by Michael Slusser, Fathers of the Church 98 (1998)

Anti-Apollinarian Writings, translated by Robin Orton, Fathers of the Church 131 (2015)

WRITINGS OF ST. GREGORY OF NYSSA IN THE FATHERS OF THE CHURCH: SHORTER WORKS SERIES

On the Six Days of Creation, translated by Robin Orton, Fathers of the Church: Shorter Works 1 (2021)